The Secret Power of
LOVE

THE BOOK OF RUTH

Other books in the growing Faithgirlz!™ library

Bibles
The Faithgirlz! Bible
NIV Faithgirlz! Backpack Bible

Bible Studies
Secret Power of Love
Secret Power of Joy
Secret Power of Goodness
Secret Power of Grace

Nonfiction
Faithgirlz Journal
The Faithgirlz! Handbook
Food, Faith & Fun: The Faithgirlz! Cookbook
No Boys Allowed
What's A Girl To Do?
Girlz Rock
Chick Chat
Real Girls of the Bible
Faithgirlz! Whatever
My Beautiful Daughter
Beauty Lab
Body Talk
Everybody Tells Me to Be Myself, But I Don't Know Who I Am
Girl Politics

Fiction

From Sadie's Sketchbook
Shades of Truth (Book One)
Flickering Hope (Book Two)
Waves of Light (Book Three)
Brilliant Hues (Book Four)

Boarding School Mysteries
Vanished (Book One)
Betrayed (Book Two)
Burned (Book Three)
Poisoned (Book Four)

Sophie's World
Sophie's World
Sophie's Secret
Sophie Under Pressure
Sophie Steps Up
Sophie's First Dance
Sophie's Stormy Summer
Sophie's Friendship Fiasco
Sophie and the New Girl
Sophie Flakes Out
Sophie Loves Jimmy
Sophie's Drama
Sophie Gets Real

The Girls of Harbor View
Girl Power
Take Charge
Raising Faith
Secret Admirer

The Lucy Series
Lucy Doesn't Wear Pink (Book One)
Lucy Out of Bounds (Book Two)
Lucy's Perfect Summer (Book Three)
Lucy Finds Her Way (Book Four)

Check out www.faithgirlz.com

faiThGirLz!
BIBLE
STUDY

The Secret Power of
LOVE

THE BOOK OF RUTH

Susie Shellenberger

ZONDERVAN®

ZONDERVAN.com/
AUTHORTRACKER
follow your favorite authors

ZONDERKIDZ

The Secret Power of Love
Copyright © 2012 by Susie Shellenberger

Illustrations © 2012 by Zonderkidz

This title is also available as a Zondervan ebook.
Visit www.zondervan.com/ebooks

Requests for information should be addressed to:
Zonderkidz, 5300 Patterson Ave. SE, Grand Rapids, Michigan 49530

ISBN 978-0-310-72838-2

All Scripture quotations, unless otherwise indicated, are taken from the Holy Bible,
New International Version®, NIV®. Copyright © 1973, 1978, 1984, 2011 by Biblica, Inc.™
Used by permission. All rights reserved worldwide.

Any Internet addresses (websites, blogs, etc.) and telephone numbers printed in this
book are offered as a resource. They are not intended in any way to be or imply an
endorsement by Zondervan, nor does Zondervan vouch for the content of these
sites and numbers for the life of this book.

Published in association with the literary agency of Alive Communica-
tions, Inc., 7680 Goddard Street, Suite 200, Colorado Springs, CO 80920.
www.alivecommunications.com

Zonderkidz is a trademark of Zondervan.

Cover design: Kris Nelson
Interior design: Sarah Molegraaf

Printed in the United States of America

12 13 14 15 16 17 18 19 /DCI/ 19 18 17 16 15 14 13 12 11 10 9 8 7 6 5 4 3 2 1

Dedicated to
Lenny and Joy Wishart.
Thanks for your friendship and prayers.

Table of Contents

Introduction

READ THIS FIRST!

Jacki's parents had decided to get a divorce. Even though she had pleaded with them to try to make it work one more time, their decision was final.

Jacki wrote in her journal:

I'm crushed. I feel like my heart is broken into so many pieces it'll be impossible to put back together again. I'm hurting, God!

Jacki couldn't fight the tears any longer. She closed her journal and threw herself across her bed. "God, are you there?" she prayed. "I need help. I need hope. I need you!"

Have you ever felt this way? Has the world ever caved in on you? Whether or not you can identify with Jacki's family situation, I bet you can understand feelings of confusion and despair.

Guess what! The book of Ruth is a book of hope. It proves that God wants to make beautiful things happen through devastating circumstances. Only *God* can take a life full of doubts, questions, and hopelessness and transform it into a life full of promise, love, and purpose. That's what God did for Ruth. And that's exactly what God wants to do for *you* too! The more you read and study God's Word and consider God's desire for love in your life, the more you will be able to discern his deep love for you and for all of us.

The "Secret Power Girls" are female Christians who are plugged into an incredible power source. In fact, you could say it's a supernatural power source. The power of the Holy Spirit. And it's available to all Christians.

When you become a Secret Power Girl and understand more about the Holy Spirit, then you can start growing stronger in your faith and deepening your relationship with Jesus. *The Secret Power of Love* takes an in-depth look at the book of Ruth, and compares her relationship with Naomi to the relationships in your own life, including your relationship with Jesus.

It's definitely okay and normal to have questions and doubts, and it's definitely good to seek out the truth. The best place for Christians to find answers is straight from the source—God's Word, the Holy Bible, and from other Christians that have gone before us and asked the same questions, like Ruth, Naomi, and Boaz.

Within the Secret Power Bible Studies, all the

information is broken up into bite-size chunks. Try to finish one BITE at every sitting, and once you've finished an entire section, you might want to get together with friends or a small Bible study group to discuss what you learned.

You can either do this study alone, with a friend, or you can ask an adult female to lead a small group of four or five girls that will meet weekly to complete the study. Another benefit of a small group is that it can help keep you accountable. Accountability means that you allow another person or small group of people to pray with you and for you, and to ask you questions about the tough stuff in your life to help you stay on the right track spiritually.

What girl doesn't need something like that?

Don't wait!

Don't accept substitutes when you can have real, unconditional love. Jesus Christ is definitely the real thing! He always has been and always will be!

So pull on your hiking boots. We're about to take an exciting journey through the book of Ruth.

Your Secret Power Sister,

Susie Shellenberger

A Move, Two Weddings, Three Funerals, & Another Move

Ruth 1: 1–22

RUTH

Where is it? Ruth is the eighth book in the Old Testament. You can find it between Judges and 1 Samuel. It's a tiny book with only 85 verses, but it's packed with a powerful message that ministers to everyone who feels left out or hopeless or who is looking for love.

Who wrote it? Lots of people think Samuel wrote it, but there are hints that Ruth was written after Samuel died. So we're not actually sure who the author is.

To whom is this letter written? It was specifically written to the people of Israel. But we can also say it was written to us because everything in the Bible is relevant forever.

The scene: This book was written during a dark and evil time in the history of Israel. Most people didn't care about pleasing God; they were only interested in themselves. Sound like today's news?

Sounds kinda like: a Cinderella story. One of the main characters—Ruth—goes from poverty to great wealth, from great sadness as a widow to great delight as the wife of an incredibly wonderful man.

BITE #1

In the days when the judges ruled, there was a famine in the land. So a man from Bethlehem in Judah, together with his wife and two sons, went to live for a while in the country of Moab.

Ruth 1:1

Israel had **no kings** at this point in its history. Judges ruled the nation. Before we go any further with this verse, let's take a step backward to the book in the Old Testament before Ruth. That book is Judges. It ends with some of the most horrific scenes in the Bible. Why? Because people were only interested in themselves.

Let's take a look at Judges 17:6: "In those days Israel had no king; everyone did as they saw fit."

What's the *problem* with doing whatever we want?

_____

_____

_____

You can imagine the **chaotic** conditions that permeated Israel during a time when everyone was doing their own thing! Some Bible commentators have called the last few chapters of Judges the "sewage of Scripture." This section of the Bible contains physical mutilation, rape, murder, and other horrendous acts.

But interestingly, immediately following the book of Judges, we find the book of Ruth—filled with **hope** and **promise**. What a stark contrast to what Israel had been experiencing. As Christians we need to remember that even in the darkest days, God can provide hope and **healing**.

Describe a time when you were in the midst of dark days yet experienced God's hope, healing, and promise.

_____

_____

_____

_____

_____

_____

> The man's name was Elimelek, his wife's name was Naomi, and the names of his two sons were Mahlon and Kilion. They were Ephrathites from Bethlehem, Judah. And they went to Moab and lived there.
>
> Ruth 1:2

We're told this family is Ephrathite. *Ephrath* is a word often linked with Bethlehem. Places where *Ephrath* is used throughout the Bible suggest there was an **importance**, or a special dignity, to being an Ephrathite. Because it's used to describe this particular family, they may have been a well-established family. Perhaps the family was wealthy or held **prestige** among their neighbors.

This verse also talks about a move. Have you ever moved to a new city?

_____ Yes

_____ No

If so, what was the most difficult part of your transition?

_____

_____

_____

_____

_____

Question to Ponder

**Think about the transition—or change—you experience
when you begin a new school year. You enter new classes
and encounter new subjects. What's the toughest part of
this transition?**

_____

_____

_____

_____

_____

_____

_____

_____

_____

_____

_____

_____

_____

_____

BITE #2

Let's think about the Ephrathites' move for a moment—
where they're from and where they're going. They're
living in the country of Judah, in the city of Bethlehem.
Bethlehem means "house of bread."

Let's enter an imaginary world for a moment. Pretend
you live in a house than cranks out fresh, hot bread every
single morning. You can choose whatever kind of bread
you want.

**Jot down the kind of bread you would choose for the
following:**

Breakfast: _____

Sandwich: _____

Simply to snack on: _____

Again, *Bethlehem* means "house of bread" and it's the
city where Jesus would be born centuries later.

**Choose the letter that best describes the connection
between Jesus and "house of bread."**

_____a. Bethlehem is the "house of bread," and Jesus
lived on bread alone.

_____b. Jesus ate only bread for the first five years of
his life.

_____ c. Bethlehem is the "house of bread," and Jesus is the Bread of Life.

_____ d. Jesus ate a lot of raisin bread.

Judah means "praise." So this family is living in the city of **bread** in the midst of **praise**. Sounds like a great place! And we can assume the family described in Ruth 1:2 is happy. Take a look at their names and what their names mean:

Elimelek: "God is my King"

Naomi: "Pleasant"

Have you ever seen those miniature license plates in novelty stores with people's first names on them? Or plaques in Hallmark stores featuring a person's name and what that name means? Our names are important! And the business executives who create money-making products know this. That's why they've created all kinds of novelty items with our names on them. They know we like to purchase things that display our name.

Do you know what your name means?

_____

_____

_____

_____

How does your name describe *you*?

_____

_____

_____

Why would a happy family choose to leave such a **great** place and journey to Moab? They left Bethlehem, Judah, when a **famine** hit the land. *But how could a famine hit such a wonderful place,* you may be thinking, *a place filled with praise for God?* Let's take a quick peek at 2 Chronicles 7:19–20:

"But if you turn away and forsake the decrees and commands I have given you and go off to serve other gods and worship them, then I will uproot Israel from my land, which I have given them, and will reject this temple I have consecrated for my Name."

In this passage we learn that if people turn away from God . . .

_____ a. God may take the Israelites' land away or force them to move.

_____ b. God probably won't notice.

_____ c. they'll never eat bread again.

_____ d. they'll only have bread to eat the rest of their lives.

Susie Shellenberger

List the two things God warns the people not to do in the above passage.

1. _____

2. _____

What does it mean to serve other gods?

_____

_____

_____

List some *idols* that Christians often let slip into their lives. (Remember—an idol is anything in your life that becomes *as* important as God or *more* important than God.)

_____

_____

_____

What idol have you struggled with?

_____

_____

_____

Let's also look at 2 Chronicles 7:14:

"If my people, who are called by my name, will humble themselves and pray and seek my face and turn from their wicked ways, then I will hear from heaven, and I will forgive their sin and will heal their land."

This verse lists *four* things that we must do to draw near to God when we have *fallen away* or walked away from God. What are they?

1. _____

2. _____

3. _____

4. _____

Have you experienced a time when you walked away from God but came back to him later? If so, describe the situation. Why did you walk away? How did you feel when you returned to him? What did you learn?

_____

_____

_____

_____

_____

Question to Ponder

And what is the promise when we come back to God?

_____

_____

_____

_____

_____

_____

_____

_____

_____

_____

_____

_____

_____

_____

BITE #3

Back to the story in Ruth. Evidently people in the city of bread and the place of praise are turning away from God. It may have been in subtle ways at first, but there *is* a turning away from God. The result?

_____ a. No more popcorn.

_____ b. Schools closed.

_____ c. Shopping malls shut down.

_____ d. Famine.

Whenever we turn away from God, we can always expect a **famine**—a dry time. We can expect to experience a famine when God doesn't have the proper place in our lives. But there is more than one kind of famine.

Check out Amos 8:11:

"The days are coming," declares the Sovereign LORD, "when I will send a famine through the land—not a famine of food or a thirst for water, but a famine of hearing the words of the Lord."

Can you *relate* to this kind of famine? Identify a time in your life when you felt like you weren't hearing from God—a time when God felt distant, a time when you felt like saying, "God, where are you? Are you even listening to me?"

_____

_____

_____

All of us will experience times of spiritual famine. The issue becomes: What will you do when spiritually dry times hit? We learn from 2 Chronicles that the **cure** for famine is to wait where you are and call on God. This is where many people jump the gun. Instead of humbling themselves, calling on God, and **waiting** for God's response and direction, they immediately seek a fast-food buffet of spiritual excitement.

They become church hoppers, or they float from one set of friends to another, or they read a variety of spiritual books—when they should simply keep reading the **Bible**, continue calling on God for help, and wait for God's guidance.

Instead of waiting out the famine, Elimelek and his family move to Moab. Grab your Bible and flip to Psalm 108:9.

How is Moab described?

_____

_____

_____

_____

Think about this picture: A godly family leaves the city of bread and the place of praise and moves to a garbage dump, a washbasin.

What other Bible story reminds you of this?

_____ a. Jesus heals a blind man.

_____ b. Jesus raises Lazarus from the dead.

_____ c. The prodigal son leaves a wonderful home and eats with pigs in a pigpen.

_____ d. Jesus heals a deaf man.

You might consider this the story of a prodigal **family**. When famine hits their land, they leave. Perhaps they get scared and let fear rule their decisions instead of **faith**. This is only one of thirteen famines mentioned in the Bible. Each time there's a famine in the Bible, it's presented as a judgment from God.

Elimelek and his family should **trust** God to take care of them. They should wait out the famine, continually humbling themselves before the Lord. But instead they flee to the land of **Moab**.

Susie Shellenberger

Question to Ponder

Can you identify a time when you should have *trusted* God, but instead you became impatient or frightened and acted on your own without waiting on God?

_____

_____

_____

_____

_____

_____

_____

_____

_____

_____

_____

_____

_____

BITE #4

Now Elimelek, Naomi's husband, died, and she was left
with her two sons.

Ruth 1:3

**Have you ever lost a loved one through *death*? If yes,
describe who died, how it happened, and the hurt you
experienced. If not, describe the hurt you felt when
someone close to you moved away or left.**

_____

_____

_____

Let's keep reading and find out what the sons do after
their father dies.

They married Moabite women, one named Orpah and
the other Ruth.

Ruth 1:4

When Naomi's sons marry Moabite women, they
immediately break the Mosaic law—the Old Testament
law. They are intermarrying with a foreign people, and
God had warned them against doing so (Numbers 36).

Look at the **downhill progression** of this family. It
starts with impatience and an unwillingness to humble
themselves and to seek and wait on the Lord. Then they

move against God's will to a place exactly the opposite of being in the city of bread and the house of praise. They move to an **ungodly** environment and set up home.

Remember what Elimelek's name means?

_____ a. My iPod rules.

_____ b. God is my King.

_____ c. My cell phone is better than yours.

_____ d. God scares me.

It's extremely tough to live out **"God is my King"** in an ungodly environment where we can't surround ourselves with godly people and enter into God's house of praise. Elimelek has moved his family to the **garbage dump** of cities.

Life has become extremely difficult; Elimelek dies. And probably because he has taken his sons away from the house of praise, God's **laws** aren't as important to them anymore. They aren't **connected** with other believers. Their **morals** have slipped, and they break the Old Testament law by **compromising** and marrying women who worship foreign gods. When we no longer hang around godly people who share our faith and our standards, it becomes very tough to continue to live a godly life with high standards.

Write down the name of someone who's tough for you to be around and be a good Christian.

_____

_____

Pray silently right now for him or her.

List someone you hang out with who encourages you to live a godly life and maintain high standards.

_____

_____

Now pray silently for him or her and thank God for putting this person in your life.

What does it mean to _compromise_?

_____

_____

_____

Describe a time in your life when _you_ compromised.

_____

_____

_____

What were the consequences?

_____

_____

_____

What things tempt us to compromise our relationship with Christ? Circle all that apply and list others that come to your mind.

peer pressure

chocolate chip cookies

God's Love

Wanting our own way

non-Christian friends

secrets

temptation

impatience

fear

lust

reading the Bible

seeking God's direction

memorizing Scripture

a strong prayer life

skipping church

other: _____

faith

Sometimes we're tempted to think we can **hide** our compromises from God. But the Bible tells us God sees and knows everything. Grab your Bible and turn to Hebrews 4:13 and paraphrase (rewrite) this passage in your own words:

_____

_____

_____

Write an email prayer in the space below telling God you don't want to compromise. Ask God to help you stand firm during tough times and not give in to the temptation to compromise.

Question to Ponder

**What are some of the characteristics you want in a
friend? Compare those with the characteristics God
desires you to have, so you can be a good friend.**

_____

_____

_____

_____

_____

_____

_____

_____

_____

_____

_____

_____

_____

_____

_____

BITE #5

> After they had lived there about ten years, both Mahlon and Kilion also died, and Naomi was left without her two sons and her husband.
>
> Ruth 1:4–5

Ten years pass. Naomi may feel as though she's lost everything. If we don't keep God in the **priority** position in our lives, when tough times come, it's easy to feel as if we've lost everything. It's easy to get **discouraged**. Naomi still has her faith in God; she simply needs to activate it and recharge her relationship with God.

When you realize you're not where you should be spiritually, what should you do to **recharge** your relationship with Christ? (There are actually four things you should do, and you can get the answers from recapping 2 Chronicles 7:14, BITE #2 on page 25.)

1. _____

2. _____

3. _____

4. _____

> When Naomi heard in Moab that the LORD had come to the aid of his people by providing food for them, she and her daughters-in-law prepared to return home from there.
>
> Ruth 1:6

The famine has **ended** in Bethlehem. The city of bread is filled with praise once again, and Naomi wants to **return** to the place she knows she should have been all along—the city of Bethlehem in the country of Judah.

Circle your three favorite breads:

wheat bread

white bread

sourdough bread

raisin bread

bread pudding

homemade bread

cinnamon bread

gingerbread

rye bread

French bread

garlic bread

multigrain bread

Now circle some of your favorite things to put on bread:

peanut butter

ice cream

honey

jelly

chicken

cereal

snails

other _____

Naomi remembers what life was like in the city of bread and the house of praise. No doubt she has kept those memories alive in her mind and turned to them often during times of grief and depression.

It's important to **remember** where we've come from. Check out Deuteronomy 5:15. The children of Israel were God's chosen people. At one time they were slaves to Pharaoh, but God delivered them and led them to a very

special place called the Promised Land—an area with
great soil for growing lots of fruits and veggies—which
was full of promise and potential.

What does Moses instruct the children of Israel to do?

_____

_____

_____

_____

**Now flip over to Deuteronomy 8:2. What does Moses
instruct the children of Israel to do?**

_____

_____

_____

_____

**Now turn back to Exodus 13:3. What is Moses asking
the people to remember?**

_____

_____

_____

_____

Question to Ponder

Take a moment to *remember* your life before you met Christ and sought forgiveness for your sins. What's the biggest *difference* in your life now versus then?

_____

_____

_____

_____

_____

_____

_____

_____

_____

_____

_____

_____

_____

_____

_____

BITE #6

With her two daughters-in-law she left the place where
she had been living and set out on the road that would
take them back to the land of Judah.

Ruth 1:7

Naomi is headed home. We can only imagine the
excitement and **peace** she feels as she pursues the road
that will lead her to where she knows God wants her to be.

Think of a time when you were away from home for a
while. Perhaps it was camp, a mission trip, or a visit to
relatives.

How did it feel when you finally got back to your home?

_____

_____

_____

_____

**What three things do you miss most when you're away
from your home?**

1. _____

2. _____

3. _____

> Then Naomi said to her two daughters-in-law, "Go back, each of you, to your mother's home. May the Lord show you kindness, as you have shown kindness to your dead husbands and to me. May the Lord grant that each of you will find rest in the home of another husband."
>
> *Ruth 1:8–9*

Naomi isn't bitter. No doubt she has **grieved** the death of her husband and her two sons, but it's clear that she wants the **best** for her two daughters-in-law.

> Then she kissed them goodbye and they wept aloud and said to her, "We will go back with you to your people."
>
> *Ruth 1:9–10*

The above verses indicate they have been a *close* family. How would you describe *your* family?

_____

_____

_____

Are there specific times or activities that make you feel closer to your family?

_____

_____

_____

But Naomi said, "Return home, my daughters. Why would you come with me? Am I going to have any more sons, who could become your husbands? Return home, my daughters; I am too old to have another husband. Even if I thought there was still hope for me—even if I had a husband tonight and then gave birth to sons—would you wait until they grew up? Would you remain unmarried for them? No, my daughters. It is more bitter for me than for you, because the Lord's hand has turned against me!"

Ruth 1:11–13

This scene has the makings of a great **chick flick**. It's filled with emotion, honesty, and wonderful dialogue. Naomi is basically telling Ruth and Orpah that she has lost **everything** in Moab. She has nothing, and she'll return to nothing in Bethlehem. Her love for her daughters-in-law (who probably seem like actual daughters to her by now) motivates her to encourage them to seek their own **happiness**.

Naomi knows the problems her girls will face if they return to Bethlehem, Judah, with her. Moabites and Israelites don't have anything to do with one another. Her daughters-in-law will face rejection, gossip, and **hardship** if they return with her to Bethlehem.

Imagine yourself in Ruth's or Orpah's shoes. How would you have responded to Naomi?

_____

_____

_____

_____

It's as if Naomi is saying, "Girls, you won't be able to remarry in Bethlehem. **No one will have you**. You're both young; you should remarry and have your own families. I've lost all my property. Why would you choose to return with me? You'll experience **poverty** and **widowhood** the rest of your life. If you come with me, the cost is high. **It will cost you everything.**"

What's the parallel between what Naomi is telling Ruth and Orpah and what Christ tells us?

_____ a. If we follow Christ, we can't get married.

_____ b. If we follow Christ, we have to move to Bethlehem.

_____ c. If we follow Christ, it will cost us everything.

_____ d. If we follow Christ, we'll always live in poverty.

Grab your Bible and turn to Luke 14:33. What does Jesus say we must give up before we can follow him?

_____

_____

Now turn to Matthew 19:27. What does Peter say to Jesus?

_____

_____

And what is Christ's response to Peter in Matthew 19:29? What will we receive in return for following Christ?

_____

_____

_____

Have you given up everything to follow Jesus?

_____

_____

_____

Ask God to reveal any area of your life that you're still clinging to; then ask for the willingness to give that up. Tell God you're willing to empty your life completely and follow Christ with abandon!

BITE #7

At this they wept aloud again. Then Orpah kissed her mother-in-law goodbye, but Ruth clung to her.

Ruth 1:14

Why do you suppose Orpah goes back to Moab?

_____

_____

_____

_____

Orpah's name means "youthful" or "immature." Her reaction is one of an **immature** believer. No doubt Naomi not only has **kept** her faith **alive** during the past ten years in Moab, but she also has **grown** stronger in her faith. And her daughters-in-law have **witnessed** her spiritual growth **firsthand**. We're led to believe that Ruth and Orpah have grown to love Naomi so much that they have also **fallen in love** with her **God**.

But this verse shows us the **difference** between the two girls' spiritual maturity. Orpah **leaves** her newfound faith in the true God and returns to idols and false gods in Moab. Ruth, however, **refuses** to go back. She's making a clean break!

Read the following scenarios and decide if the person is making a clean break:

Becca has started gambling online. When she accepts Christ, she continues to gamble but gives some of the money she wins to her church.

Clean break? _____ Yes _____ No

Emma has sexted some messages to the guys in her class. This past week at church, however, she confessed her sins and accepted Christ into her life. When Ryan texts her asking for some more images from her phone, she texts: "No more."

Clean break? _____ Yes _____ No

Hayley often lies to her parents. Her mom has confronted her about it, but Haley figures lying doesn't really matter to God.

Clean break? _____ Yes _____ No

Is there anything you need to make a clean break from? If so, will you take a moment to pray silently right now and give that area of your life to Christ? First ask him to forgive you, then commit that problem area to him.

_____
_____
_____
_____

When we confess our sins and accept Christ's forgiveness, he expects us to walk away from our sins. He wants us to make a clean break—and he'll give us the strength to do just that!

Take another look at Ruth 1:14. What action does Orpah demonstrate with Naomi?

_____

_____

_____

What action does Ruth demonstrate?

_____

_____

_____

Do you see the difference between the two? One is expressing _emotion_; the other is expressing _devotion_. Which one does Ruth express?

_____

_____

_____

Take a moment to evaluate your emotion-versus-devotion factor. Mark each of the following statements **true** or **false**.

I tend to express my love for God mostly through emotion.

_____ True _____ False

I tend to express my love for God through prayer, Bible reading, and obedience.

_____ True _____ False

If I'm not surrounded by other Christians, I often question my faith in God.

_____ True _____ False

If I can't feel God, I doubt God's existence.

_____ True _____ False

I sometimes feel God's presence, but other times I don't. My faith remains consistent and isn't based on what I feel. I base my relationship with God on fact, not feeling.

_____ True _____ False

When God seems far away, I assume God *is* far away.

_____ True _____ False

When God seems far away, I still believe God is with me because of the promise that God will never leave me.

_____ True _____ False

My relationship with Christ tends to revolve around my emotions—what I'm feeling and how I'm feeling.

_____ True _____ False

My relationship with Christ is based on the fact that I have chosen to follow him whether I feel his presence or not.

_____ True _____ False

Think about your **own** relationship with Christ. When you're surrounded by other Christians (church camp, retreats, Bible study, youth group, etc.), it's easy to get caught up in expressing **emotion**. But eventually you have to come down off the spiritual mountaintop. So what happens when camp is **over**?

What happens when the **emotion** is gone, the **music** has faded, and your **friends** have gone their separate ways? If your relationship with Christ is based on **emotion**, it won't last long. But if you've grounded your relationship with Jesus on **devotion**, it can surely weather the hard times. It will be **real** and **lasting**.

What's the difference between demonstrating emotion and demonstrating devotion?

_____

_____

_____

Orpah kisses Naomi, but Ruth clings to her. Orpah is close to her mother-in-law, but Ruth has become a part of her life. Describe the difference between being close to Christ and actually becoming one with him.

_____

_____

Question to Ponder

Are you close to Christ—simply living next to him? Or are you attaching yourself to him and enjoying the process of becoming part of him?

_____

_____

_____

_____

_____

_____

_____

_____

_____

_____

_____

_____

_____

BITE #8

"Look," said Naomi, "your sister-in-law is going back to her people and her gods. Go back with her."

But Ruth replied, "Don't urge me to leave you or to turn back from you. Where you go I will go, and where you stay I will stay. Your people will be my people and your God my God."

Ruth 1:15–16

Ruth has clearly **decided** to forsake all idols and false gods for Naomi's true God. Evidently, she sees so much **fruit** of a growing, active relationship with God in Naomi's life, she can't help but desire the same thing.

What *evidences* of God do you hope people see in *your* life?

_____

_____

_____

Let's look at the **fruit of the Spirit** that God wants to cultivate in every believer's life.

But the fruit of the Spirit is love, joy, peace, forbearance, kindness, goodness, faithfulness, gentleness and self-control.

Galatians 5:22–23

Which of these fruits are demonstrated in Naomi's life with her daughters-in-law?

_____

_____

_____

Circle the following fruits that are most evident in your life:

kindness   gentleness

self-control   joy   Love

patience   faithfulness

goodness   peace

Circle the following fruits that are least evident in your life:

kindness   gentleness

self-control   joy   Love

patience   faithfulness

goodness   peace

Prayer

Ask God to help you cultivate **each** fruit of the Spirit in your life.

_____

_____

_____

_____

_____

_____

_____

_____

_____

_____

_____

_____

_____

_____

BITE #9

"Where you die I will die, and there I will be buried. May the LORD deal with me, be it ever so severely, if even death separates you and me."

Ruth 1:17

What similarities do you see between Ruth's devotion to Naomi and a Christian's devotion to Christ?

_____

_____

_____

Ruth makes a seven-part commitment to Naomi. Complete the statements that show each commitment she makes:

Where you go _____ .

Where you stay _____ .

Your people _____ .

Your God _____ .

Where you die _____ ,

and there _____ .

May the Lord deal with me, _____ ,
if even death separates you and me.

What a commitment! Let's look in turn at each **part** of Ruth's commitment.

One: When Ruth says she'll go with Naomi, she isn't simply seeking a **passport** out of the garbage dump to the city of bread. When you **first** made a commitment to Christ, it may have been so you could have the assurance of going to **heaven** or escaping **hell**. But as you grow in your relationship with him, you begin to fall in love with Christ. Though you look forward to being with Christ forever in heaven, you also enjoy your relationship with him **right now**.

List three things you love about your relationship with Christ right now:

1. _____

2. _____

3. _____

List three things you're looking forward to experiencing in heaven:

1. _____

2. _____

3. _____

Two: Next Ruth says she'll **stay** with Naomi when they arrive in Bethlehem. In other words, Ruth is willing to **identify** with Naomi and her poverty. She isn't planning to forsake the old woman to seek her own riches. She's not going to Bethlehem, Judah, to chase guys; she's going to be a part of Naomi's **life** and serve Naomi's **God**.

Christ wants you to identify with him. In the *Secret Power of Grace* Bible study of 1 Peter, we discuss how we can identify with Christ when we go through times of trials and suffering. In what other areas of your life can you identify with your Savior? For example, do you show others unconditional love? Do you demonstrate kindness, gentleness, patience, and self-control?

_____

_____

_____

_____

_____

_____

Three: Ruth claims that Naomi's **people** will become her own people. She's willing to leave **behind** the friendships and relationships that have kept her from becoming all God wants her to be.

Have you had to give up a friendship or relationship because it was hindering your relationship with Christ? If so, describe that. If not, describe what you think that would be like.

_____

_____

_____

_____

_____

Is there a friendship or relationship you **need** to give up to become all that God wants you to be? If so, describe that. Why? Is it hard to end that relationship? Why or why not?

_____

_____

_____

_____

_____

Four: Ruth also claims that Naomi's **God** will be her God. She's **forsaking** idols and other gods and those who worship them so she can give her life to God Almighty.

What have you forsaken to follow Christ with all your life? Maybe avoiding certain movies, television shows, or video games.

_____

_____

_____

_____

Five: Ruth is determined to **die** in the same land where Naomi will die. This proves Ruth's commitment isn't temporary. She's thinking ahead—even unto death.

When we give Christ our **all**, we die (in a sense) to our rights, our wills, and our own selfish desires. Grab your Bible and turn to Galatians 2:20.

What does the apostle Paul claim has happened to him?

_____

_____

_____

Six: Ruth claims she will be **buried** in the place she will die (in Bethlehem, Judah, where Naomi will also die—rather than in Moab, where Ruth is from and would've been buried if she had stayed).

How does this prove that her commitment isn't a spur-of-the-moment emotional promise? How does her intention to be buried where she will die make her commitment genuine?

_____

_____

_____

_____

Seven: Ruth is so **serious** about her commitment that she seals it by asking God to deal severely with her if she ever breaks it.

How would a similar prayer or covenant change the commitment of many Christians?

_____

_____

_____

_____

Ruth concludes her seven-part pledge to Naomi by telling her that nothing besides **death** will separate her from her mother-in-law. Many Christians would let a lot **less** than death separate them from God. Many have easily turned their backs on God and given up their faith.

List some things people allow to separate them from God.

_____

_____

_____

_____

_____

_____

Have you known someone who has "thrown in the towel"—or given up—on their relationship with Christ? Why do you suppose they did that? What will keep you from doing that?

_____

_____

_____

_____

_____

_____

When Naomi realized that Ruth was determined to go with her, she stopped urging her.

Ruth 1:18

Question to Ponder

Naomi realizes Ruth is extremely serious about her commitment to God. What can other people see— proven by your lifestyle—that shows you're serious about your commitment to Christ?

_____

_____

_____

_____

_____

_____

_____

_____

_____

_____

_____

_____

BITE #10

So the two women went on until they came to Bethlehem. When they arrived in Bethlehem, the whole town was stirred because of them, and the women exclaimed, "Can this be Naomi?"

Ruth 1:19

Finally! The prodigal family returns home to Bethlehem. But it's not an entire family any longer; it's simply Naomi and Ruth. Think of a time when you were **away** from home for a while and describe what your **return** was like. It has been ten years since Naomi's friends have seen her. Imagine the excitement at this **reunion**!

"Don't call me Naomi," she told them. "Call me Mara, because the Almighty has made my life very bitter. I went away full, but the Lord has brought me back empty. Why call me Naomi? The Lord has afflicted me; the Almighty has brought misfortune upon me."

Ruth 1:20–21

Remember—Naomi's name means "**pleasant**." She left Bethlehem with a husband and two sons. She had a **full** life. But she has returned a widow with a foreign daughter-in-law who is also a widow. It's obvious that Naomi has **suffered** a great deal in the past ten years.

But when we *choose* to leave the city of bread and the house of praise—when we choose to walk away from where God has placed us—we should **expect** rough times. The Bible is clear that God will **discipline** us when needed.

What's the advantage of being disciplined?

_____

_____

_____

When someone disciplines me, what does it prove?

_____ a. That person hates me.

_____ b. That person loves me enough to help me see that what I did was wrong and is willing to help me correct it.

_____ c. I never really was a Christian.

_____ d. I can't do anything right.

Let's check out Hebrews 12:5–6:

Have you completely forgotten this word of encouragement that addresses you as a father addresses his son? It says, "My son, do not make light of the Lord's discipline, and do not lose heart when he rebukes you, because the Lord disciplines the one he loves, and he chastens everyone he accepts as his son."

According to the above passage, what two things is God proving to you when he disciplines you?

1. _____

2. _____

Now let's look at Hebrews 12:7:

Endure hardship as discipline; God is treating you as his children. For what children are not disciplined by their father?

According to this verse, how might Naomi view her hardship?

_____

_____

_____

Now read Hebrews 12:10:

[Our fathers] disciplined us for a little while as they thought best; but God disciplines us for our good, in order that we may share in his holiness.

According to this verse, God disciplines us for which two reasons?

1. _____

2. _____

Now grab your Bible and read Hebrews 12:11. What two things will result from God's discipline in our lives?

1. _____

2. _____

Question to Ponder

Think about a time when you were disciplined— either by your parents or by God—and what you learned from it.

_____

_____

_____

_____

_____

_____

_____

_____

_____

_____

BITE #11

Back to Naomi. She tells her friends to call her **Mara**—which means "sad" or "gloomy." You'd think her friends would see her plight and do what she suggests—call her Mara. **But they don't.** Check out the last verse in chapter one:

> So Naomi returned from Moab accompanied by Ruth the Moabite, her daughter-in-law, arriving in Bethlehem as the barley harvest was beginning.
>
> Ruth 1:22

Who returns? *Naomi.* Her friends refuse to let Naomi's situation label her lifestyle. Because her friends have strong relationships with **God**, they see the same potential in Naomi that God sees—promise, hope, and fulfillment.

When *you've* been disciplined, experienced rough times, and feel empty, you may be tempted to allow your actions to reflect your feelings. **Don't!** Jesus always sees your **potential**. Christ focuses on what you **can become** with his help. And he wants you to focus on his **restoration** in your life as well!

Describe a time in your life when you felt *discouraged* and empty yet someone else was able to help you focus on the *bright* side.

_____

_____

GRAB A FRIEND

Congrats! You made it through the first chapter of Ruth. Now grab a friend and discuss the following questions together:

@ In the first bite we looked at Judges 17:6: "In those days Israel had no king; everyone did as they saw fit." Has there been a time this past week when I wanted my own way but did what was right instead?

@ What have I done this past week to ensure I don't experience a spiritual famine?

@ Is there any area of my life in which I compromised this week?

@ How have I shown the fruit of the Spirit in my life this week?

Memorize It!

Try to memorize this verse with your friend and say it to each other the next time you get together.

"Where you go I will go, and where you stay I will stay. Your people will be my people and your God my God. Where you die I will die, and there I will be buried."

Ruth 1:16–17

My Journal

Okay, Secret Power Girl. This is your space, so take advantage of it. You can do whatever you want with this space but always try to include the following:

@ List your prayer requests. (Later, as God answers them, go back and record the dates when God answered your prayers.)

@ Copy down any verse we studied in the previous chapter that you don't understand. Then let this be a reminder to ask your parents, Sunday school teacher, pastor, or youth leader about it.

@ Jot down what stood out most to you from this chapter.

SECTION TWO

Girl Meets Guy

Ruth 2:1–23

Now Naomi had a relative on her husband's side, a man of standing from the clan of Elimelek, whose name was Boaz.

And Ruth the Moabite said to Naomi, "Let me go to the fields and pick up the leftover grain behind anyone in whose eyes I find favor."

Ruth 2:1–2

We get some **important** information in this first verse. As readers, we're being let in on a *secret*. Most books don't reveal their secrets until the last chapter, but here we learn that Boaz is a relative—a **guardian**—of Naomi.

That will take on great significance in this book—in fact, the rest of the story will revolve around this secret—but we'll save that for later.

The name **Boaz** means "standing in strength." He's an impressive man with an important heritage. He comes from the tribe of **Judah**. From Boaz would come David, and eventually the King of Kings (Jesus Christ) would come from this same line.

Grab your Bible and turn to 1 Kings 7:21. Read this passage to find out what David's son **Solomon** names after his impressive great-great-grandfather Boaz.

If you could designate something to be named after you, what would you select and why? (Try to think of something that would reflect your personality or your character.)

_____

_____

_____

_____

_____

We also learn from this passage that **Ruth** doesn't tag along with Naomi, expecting her mother-in-law to provide for her. She's not along for a free ride. She's willing to **work**. This speaks highly of Ruth's **character**.

Ruth was a hard worker. Let's evaluate your work ethic.

When I'm given a job, I always do my very best.

_____ True _____ False

I usually work harder when someone is watching.

_____ True _____ False

I work harder in school than I do with household chores.

_____ True _____ False

If I'm not getting paid, I don't work as hard.

_____ True _____ False

I get tired out easily, so I'm not much of a worker.

_____ True _____ False

Susie Shellenberger *reputation*

Think about your own character for a moment. If an adult outside your family (pastor, youth leader, school teacher, etc.) were asked to describe your character, what would he or she say?

_____

_____

_____

_____

What would help you achieve a better work ethic?

_____

_____

_____

_____

Is it important to be a hard worker? Why or why not?

_____

_____

_____

talk out load

passage 10:4-5 primove at some

Naomi said to her, "Go ahead, my daughter." So she went out, entered a field and began to glean behind the harvesters.

Boaz hire workers they called harvesters the sheaves

Ruth 2:2-8

80

taking what harvesters didn't get

The **gleaning** issue was part of a strange law. It's mentioned in Leviticus 19:9–10:

"When you reap the harvest of your land, do not reap to the very edges of your field or gather the gleanings of your harvest. Do not go over your vineyard a second time or pick up the grapes that have fallen. Leave them for the poor and the foreigner. I am the Lord your God."

This was God's way of telling the Israelites they had to take care of the poor and those from other countries. There was no welfare; food stamps weren't available; and there were no soup kitchens. So the poor were taken care of in this unusual way.

collect

They had to glean—or work for the grain—but it was free to them. This strange law is directed to the landowners and is stated again in Leviticus 23:22: *hard*

"When you reap the harvest of your land, do not reap to the very edges of your field or gather the gleanings of your harvest. Leave them for the poor and for the foreigner residing among you. I am the Lord your God."

Now grab your Bible and turn to Deuteronomy 24:19. According to this passage, what are the harvesters not to do?

Boaz @ end

You might be gathering your harvest in the field. You might see a bundle of grain. Don't go back + get it. Leave it there for the foreigner, orphans, widows. Then the Lord your God will bless you in whatever you do

This was God's **wonderful** way of caring for the needy. Instead of lining them up for charity or putting them in a breadline, God put them to **work**. Machines weren't available in those days, and gleaning by hand was extremely hard work. When the harvesters **gleaned** by hand, they left approximately 30 percent of the grain in the field. They simply couldn't get it all. And once they'd gone through the field, God told them *not* to go back and pick up the leftovers; these were to be left for the poor.

What does this tell you about God's concern for the poor?

_____

_____

_____

_____

Now that you understand a little more about the gleaning process, what does this tell you about Ruth's work ethic?

_____

_____

_____

_____

What are *you* doing to help the needy?

_____

_____

_____

_____

Question to Ponder

What are some things you and your friends could do to help the less fortunate? (Could you tutor a child, serve in a soup kitchen, sponsor a child through Compassion International, babysit free for a needy family, etc.?)

_____FISH_____

_____out loud_____

_____

_____

_____

_____

_____

BITE #2

As it turned out, she was working in a field belonging to
Boaz, who was from the clan of Elimelek.

Ruth 2:3

It's obvious that Ruth's **priorities** are right. She's not
chasing guys (though she certainly could be; she's single
and young, and it would be much easier to be taken care
of than to have to take care of herself and her mother-in-
law). She's **not** in the fields to find someone she can meet.
Ruth is working hard, and she's doing backbreaking **labor**.

Instead of hoping God will plop food in her lap, she
takes the initiative. Is there something in your life you've
been **waiting** on God for? It could be that God is waiting
on *you* to take the initiative.

According to Ruth 2:3, to whom is Boaz related?

_____

_____

**And do you remember the relation of Elimelek to
Naomi?**

_____ a. He is Naomi's third cousin on her great-
aunt's side.

_____ b. He is Naomi's servant.

Susie Shellenberger

_____ c. He is Naomi's brother.

_____ d. He is Naomi's husband.

Many laws were established long ago in different states that are no longer needed but still exist. Some are pretty funny. Take a peek at the following actual laws that still remain in the books:

» In Alabama, it's against the law to play dominoes on Sunday.

» Have you seen any giraffes walking the streets lately? Maybe that's because it's illegal to tie a giraffe to a telephone pole in Vermont.

» In Missouri, it's against the law to offer beer to an elephant.

» At one time in New York, you could be fined $25 for flirting.

» A Pennsylvania law once forbid people to sing in the bathtub.

» A parent could be arrested in Nebraska if his child burped during a church service.

» Getting a tattoo in Wisconsin was once illegal—unless it was for medical purposes.

» It's illegal in Texas to sell your eye.

86

Strange but Useful Bible Laws

Now it's time to take a look at another law. This is a strange law that God set into place to help his people. It's the special **kinsman-redeemer** law.

This kinsman-redeemer law is outlined in Leviticus 25. Here's how the law worked: God had told the people of Israel they would enter the **Promised Land** and could claim that land for themselves.

God placed them in the land according to **tribes**. A specific tribe had a certain section of the **land**. And each family within each tribe received a particular **plot** within the section.

So imagine **Mr. Smith** owns forty acres of land that has been designated to him and his family. Let's also imagine that Mr. Smith has three years of little rain and poor crops, and as a result, he's in desperate need of money. What's he going to do?

Here's where another strange law comes into play: **the Year of Jubilee**.

Let's say Mr. Smith has a **rich** neighbor, **Mr. Jones**. So Mr. Smith sells his land to Mr. Jones. They settle on a price, and instead of paying all the money up front, Mr. Jones "mortgages" the land, or pays a set amount each month plus interest, to Mr. Smith (kind of like paying rent except each payment goes toward full ownership).

But here's where it gets interesting. So you've probably heard your parents talk about the mortgage on their house.

Today a typical mortgage lasts thirty years. But in Bible times, mortgages could be spread out over a longer period of time, but the absolute longest time for a mortgage was fifty years because of another strange law known as "the Year of Jubilee." According to this law, set down by God, Mr. Jones can only take up to a fifty-year mortgage because during the Year of Jubilee every mortgage is **canceled**. The land returns to its original owner.

Strange law, huh? But this law kept land in a family. Still … it's a long wait between jubilees. Mr. Smith might be **sixty** years old when Mr. Jones offers to take his mortgage. So in fifty more years, Mr. Smith will probably be **dead**. But because the land will stay in the Smith family, the land will go to Mr. Smith's **son** in fifty years.

Now back to the kinsman-redeemer law. Assume Mr. Jones mortgaged the Smith property for fifty years, but five years later, Mr. Smith's wealthy uncle (his kinsman, or guardian) moves to town. He can pay the mortgage off and restore the land to Mr. Smith, redeeming him from the mortgage. This way Mr. Smith won't have to wait **forty-five** more years until the Year of Jubilee.

It would be terrific to have a rich uncle as a redeemer, wouldn't it? The kinsman-redeemer is a wonderful picture of our Lord Jesus Christ. He is our kinsman-redeemer. And he's the reason the word *redemption* is used in the New Testament instead of *atonement*.

Atonement simply covered up sins—that's all. But **redemption** means to pay a price so that the one who's been redeemed is able to go **free**! Jesus Christ not only died to redeem **people**, but he also died to redeem the **earth**. We live on an earth that will someday be delivered from the bondage of corruption. There will be a **new heaven** and a **new earth**; that's part of God's redemption plan, as well as his redemption of people. God has a **perfect** and wonderful way of caring for people **and** creation.

Boaz is related to Naomi's deceased husband, **Elimelek**. So **Boaz** will get a chance to become a kinsman-redeemer to **Ruth**. But we're getting ahead of ourselves. Let's slow down, back up, and keep diving into the Scriptures. We'll eventually come to the plot in this romance where the kinsman-redeemer starts to look like a **hero!**

Question to Ponder

Is there a family member you know who could benefit from the kinsman-redeemer law?

_____

_____

_____

_____

_____

_____

Susie Shellenberger

> Just then Boaz arrived from Bethlehem and greeted the harvesters, "The Lord be with you!"
>
> "The Lord bless you!" they answered.
>
> Ruth 2:4

We don't need a zoom lens to get a clear picture of Boaz's character from the above passage. Boaz is the rich guy, the landowner. He **hires** the harvesters. We could compare him to a company **president**. It's rare that the president of the organization mixes with the temps. **Boaz walks right among the workers.**

And God does the **same** with us. Our rich King—the one who created and controls the entire world—has **always** walked with people, beginning way back in the Garden of Eden.

Grab your Bible and turn to Genesis 3:8. When did God walk with Adam?

_____

_____

_____

_____

_____

_____

God also walked with people in the nation of Israel. Read Exodus 40:34–38. Where was God's glory?

_____

_____

_____

_____

_____

Then God came in the form of a human being and walked among us through the person of Jesus Christ. **Today** God still walks with us through the Holy Spirit who dwells within us. God also walks with us through the **church** (the body of Christ).

Describe three things that make you aware of God's presence.

1. _____

2. _____

3. _____

Isn't it great that you don't have to go through a lot of red tape to reach God? Christ is your bridge to the Father. Anything you ask of Jesus, he takes straight to the Father. We have access to the Creator of the universe!

How does this make you feel? (Mark all that apply.)

_____ a. Blah

_____ b. Grateful

_____ c. Excited

_____ d. Hungry

_____ e. Special

_____ f. Loved

_____ g. Ignored

_____ h. Part of God's family

The Drop Box March 21st
^

God's Not Dead 28th
^

^

Madifri's Day
Mar 11 Fri

Solace

BITE #3 *Amy resay the law thing*

Boaz asked the overseer of his harvesters, "Who does that young woman belong to?"

The overseer replied, "She is the Moabite who came back from Moab with Naomi. She said, 'Please let me glean and gather among the sheaves behind the harvesters.' She came into the field and has remained here from morning till now, except for a short rest in the shelter."

Ruth 2:5–7

It's obvious that Boaz . . .

Read Ruth 2:

_____ a. is hungry.

_____ b. is interested in finding out who Ruth is.

_____ c. is wishing he had an iPad.

_____ d. is looking for another worker.

People know who **Ruth** is. She stands out in a **good** way. Ruth doesn't simply become part of the **crowd**.

Think about yourself for a moment. Do you . . .

_____ a. stand out in a good way?

_____ b. simply become part of the crowd?

_____ c. stand out in a negative way?

Think of two things you can do to stand out in a positive way.

1. _____

2. _____

We also learn from Ruth 2:5–7 that she . . .

_____ a. works steadily.

_____ b. is a lazy bum.

_____ c. desperately wants a new cell phone.

_____ d. hates anything made with grain.

Question to Ponder

Even though the law stated that Ruth was eligible to glean behind the harvesters, she still asks permission. What does this tell you about her character?

So Boaz said to Ruth, "My daughter, listen to me. Don't go and glean in another field and don't go away from here. Stay here with the women who work for me."

Ruth 2:8

Clearly Boaz is going out of his way to make sure Ruth **knows** that not only is it okay for her to glean in his field, but he actually *wants* her to glean in his field!

Describe a time when someone went out of their way to make you feel welcome.

_____

_____

_____

_____

_____

Describe a time when you went out of your way to make someone else feel welcome.

_____

_____

_____

_____

_____

"Watch the field where the men are harvesting, and follow along after the women. I have told the men not to lay a hand on you. And whenever you are thirsty, go and get a drink from the water jars the men have filled."

Ruth 2:9

Okay, Boaz is no longer simply being courteous. He's actually watching over Ruth. He's taking care of her. He's **interested**!

Who are the people in your life who try to protect you and take care of you?

_____

_____

_____

_____

How does this make you feel?

_____

_____

_____

Notice Ruth's response to Boaz's offer of protection.

At this, she bowed down with her face to the ground. She asked him, "Why have I found such favor in your eyes that you notice me—a foreigner?"

Ruth 2:10

Ruth isn't flippant in her **gratitude**. She makes sure there is no doubt in the mind of Boaz that she's extremely appreciative. She knows he's going out of his way. She doesn't deserve such care or provision.

Describe a time when you received undeserved grace.

_____

_____

_____

_____

Ruth certainly didn't expect such a **favorable** response from such an important man as Boaz. Remember—Naomi had warned her that life in Bethlehem wouldn't be easy.

Ruth, however, was willing to make the sacrifice. And now God is **blessing** her obedience! Note that Ruth is a foreigner, but Boaz's concern and love for her break through all racial **barriers**.

The Israelites looked **down** on the Moabites. The Moabites, at times, were even shut out from the congregation of the Lord—what we might call "church."

How does Boaz remind you of Christ?

_____

_____

_____

_____

Grab your Bible and read Romans 5:8. According to this verse, when did Christ die for you?

_____

_____

_____

And according to our story in Ruth, when does Boaz show compassion toward this foreigner Ruth?

_____ a. When she's dressed in her best and well groomed

_____ b. When she's filthy, sweaty, and tired from working all day

_____ c. When she's had a fresh manicure and is wearing the latest from Bath & Body Works

_____ d. When she's had highlights put in her hair

BITE #4 A good name

Boaz replied, "I've been told all about what you have done for your mother-in-law since the death of your husband—how you left your father and mother and your homeland and came to live with a people you did not know before. May the Lord repay you for what you have done. May you be richly rewarded by the Lord, the God of Israel, under whose wings you have come to take refuge."

Ruth 2:11–12

According to the last part of the above passage, under whose wings is Ruth taking refuge?

_____

_____

_____

_____

Perhaps you've heard the phrase, "I want to be the hands and feet of Jesus." Who is being the hands and feet of God for Ruth in the above passage?

_____

_____

_____

_____

When were you the hands or feet of Christ to someone?

_____

_____

_____

_____

_____

Can you identify a time when someone was Jesus's hands or feet to you?

_____

_____

_____

_____

_____

The first part of this passage **informs** us that news about Ruth and her wonderful relationship with her mother-in-law has gotten around. People know about her. They're talking about her—and they're saying **good** things!

We're clearly told in the book of James (4:11) not to **gossip**. Gossip is usually a negative action, and that's what the apostle James warns us against. But here's an example of **positive** gossip!

Think of someone you know and list three pieces of positive gossip you can share with others about him or her.

1. _____

2. _____

3. _____

Strive to make it a good habit to **spread** positive gossip about others. God loves it when we affirm others and build them up.

By spreading positive gossip, you can (mark all that apply) . . .

_____ a. start a new trend.

_____ b. help someone feel good about himself or herself.

_____ c. contribute in a good way to someone's reputation.

_____ d. help others have a clearer view of the person about whom you're speaking.

Ruth has placed her faith in Naomi's **God**. Boaz, too, is a God-fearing man. And now that he has **met** Ruth, he realizes that all the good things he has heard about her

Susie Shellenberger

are **true**. He's deeply attracted to her, and **romance** is beginning to stir in his heart!

The best kind of relationships are those that are . . .

_____ a. based on looks.

_____ b. grounded in solid faith in Christ.

_____ c. surface-level and short-lived.

_____ d. long-distance.

What do you gain from your Christian friends that you don't get from non-Christian friends?

"May I continue to find favor in your eyes, my lord," she said. "You have put me at ease by speaking kindly to your servant—though I do not have the standing of one of your servants."

Ruth 2:13

Ruth is a *wise* woman! She doesn't let the attention from Boaz go to her head. She doesn't suddenly start thinking, *I'm all that! The big guy's got it for me.* She keeps her **perspective** and is mindful of her boundaries. She still knows that she's the worker and Boaz is the landowner.

Girls often overstep their **boundaries** at the first sign of interest from a guy. The wise young woman will surrender her dating life to God.

When you start dating, what would be the advantages of allowing God to be in charge of your dating life?

_____

_____

_____

_____

_____

_____

Question to Ponder

Have you made the commitment to put God in charge of your dating relationships? If not, do so right now.

_____

_____

_____

_____

_____

_____

BITE #5

At mealtime Boaz said to her, "Come over here. Have some bread and dip it in the wine vinegar."

When she sat down with the harvesters, he offered her some roasted grain. She ate all she wanted and had some left over.

Ruth 2:14

Notice what Boaz is offering Ruth—bread and wine vinegar—a picture of **communion**.

Jesus invites *you* to have daily communion with him. He wants you to experience spiritual **intimacy** with him as he provides for you.

Identify anything in your life that's keeping you from experiencing spiritual intimacy with God.

_____

_____

_____

How often do you commune/fellowship with God?

_____

_____

_____

Susie Shellenberger

Not only does Ruth get full, but she also has leftovers! What does this tell you about the kind of life God wants to give you?

_____ a. God wants me to eat grain.

_____ b. God not only wants to be my provider but also wants to give me a full life!

_____ c. God wants me to have dinner with a landowner.

_____ d. God wants me to eat all my meals at restaurants.

Let's take a peek at John 10:10:

"I have come that they may have life, and have it to the full."

According to this passage, what kind of life does God want you to experience?

_____

_____

_____

_____

_____

Are you living abundantly in Jesus? List some ways you can have a more abundant spiritual life.

_____

_____

_____

> As she got up to glean, Boaz gave orders to his men, "Let her gather among the sheaves and don't reprimand her. Even pull out some stalks for her from the bundles and leave them for her to pick up, and don't rebuke her."
>
> Ruth 2:15–16

In other words, Boaz tells his workers to leave some of the *best* grain right in Ruth's path so it will be easy for her to collect. If we compare this with our Christian walk, we can use this as a reminder that Christianity doesn't always have to be **difficult**. wide / narrow path

~~Many~~ Some people **complain** about what they've given up to follow Christ. hard to walk the narrow - I feel like But whatever we surrender to him is I'm the only one **nothing** in comparison to his sacrifice for us. He gave his life! **Salvation** is really quite easy. It's a free **gift** to all who will believe, accept Christ's forgiveness, and live for him.

Ruth still has to put forth an effort to **get** the grain, but she doesn't have to struggle to find it. When we ask Christ to be Lord of our lives, we receive his forgiveness for free, but we still need to put forth an effort to live in **obedience** to him.

How do we show God we ♥ Him?

Grab your Bible and flip to John 14:15. If you truly love God, what will you do?

If you love me, keep my commands

- If you love me, show it by doing what I've told you

Now read John 14:23. What good things will those who obey God experience?

My Father will love them, we'll move right into the neighborhood

Now look at John 14:24. What does Christ say about the one who doesn't obey him?

doesn't observe & obey my teachings - does@ Him

A Letter from Jesus

Read John 15:10. Insert your own name into this verse and rewrite it as a letter to yourself from Jesus.

if Abby keeps my commands, you'll remain intimately at home in my love. That's what I've done kept my Father's commands and made myself at home in His love

♡ Jesus

BITE #6

So Ruth gleaned in the field until evening. Then she threshed the barley she had gathered, and it amounted to about an ephah.

Ruth 2:17

An ephah equals one-half bushel or 22 liters. That's a lot of barley! God uses **Boaz** to provide abundantly for Ruth.

When has God abundantly provided for you?

_____

_____

_____

_____

Has God worked through any particular person to provide for you? Who?

_____

_____

_____

_____

Susie Shellenberger

Question to Ponder

Will you make a point to thank the above person who has provided for you?

_____

_____

_____

She carried it back to town, and her mother-in-law saw how much she had gathered. Ruth also brought out and gave her what she had left over after she had eaten enough.

Her mother-in-law asked her, "Where did you glean today? Where did you work? Blessed be the man who took notice of you!"

Ruth 2:18–19

Ruth brings home more than the average worker. It's obvious to Naomi that someone has been kind to Ruth. How have you shown kindness to someone less fortunate than you during the past few weeks?

_____

_____

_____

_____

Read Ruth 2:18–19 again and notice Naomi's response to what Ruth brings home. List as many words as you can that describe the variety of emotions Naomi must be feeling.

_____

_____

_____

_____

_____

Let's look at Ruth 2:18–19 one more time:

> She carried it back to town, and her mother-in-law saw how much she had gathered. Ruth also brought out and gave her what she had left over after she had eaten enough.

> Her mother-in-law asked her, "Where did you glean today? Where did you work? Blessed be the man who took notice of you!"

Ruth doesn't glean haphazardly in a scrawny field. She works steadily and gleans in the **lush** field of Boaz. When seeking a place to find food, she headed toward the **best field** she could find. She gleans right where God wants her to glean. What about **your** gleaning habits? Answer the following questions to help determine whether you're "gleaning" as you should.

When you're seeking spiritual nourishment, do you do so halfheartedly or with 100% effort?

_____

_____

_____

_____

Body, Spirit →

When seeking spiritual food, are you content to be satisfied with anything that looks or sounds good, or do you seek absolute truth?

> Follow your heart
> I just want you to be happy.
> Do what feels good

Are you more likely to "glean" from the latest movie or the Word of God when you're down and in need of encouragement?

_____

_____

_____

_____

How and where do you find spiritual nourishment?

_____

_____

_____

_____

We will eventually become what we glean or absorb. Think about the past two weeks. Have you absorbed more from the news or the Bible?

instagram, FB, ea
_____
Pinterest

_____

Are you currently gleaning where God has directed, or are you gleaning on your own?

_____

_____

_____

Then Ruth told her mother-in-law about the one at whose place she had been working. "The name of the man I worked with today is Boaz," she said.

Ruth 2:19

Ruth still doesn't know who Boaz is, but **Naomi** knows. A romance has started to bloom between the important landowner and the poor foreign widow, but she's still unaware of the fact that Boaz is related to her and probably still a bit naive in understanding his feelings toward her.

Though *you* don't see and understand everything, take comfort in the fact that God does! God knows all, sees all, and has a wonderful plan for your life.

Grab your Bible and turn to Jeremiah 29:11. What kinds of plans does God have for you?

_____

_____

_____

_____

And flip to Ephesians 3:20. According to this passage, how big does God dream for you?

God can do anything, you know—far more than you could ever imagine or guess or request in your wildest dreams! He does it not by pushing us around but by working w/in us, His Spirit deeply + gently w/in us.

Letter to God

Take a moment to write a letter of gratitude to God for knowing all, loving you more than you can comprehend, and promising to meet your needs. He is your ultimate provider!

_____

_____

_____

_____

_____

_____

_____

_____

_____

_____

_____

_____

_____

_____

_____

_____

BITE #7

"The Lord bless him!" Naomi said to her daughter-in-law. "He has not stopped showing his kindness to the living and the dead." She added, "That man is our close relative; he is one of our kinsman-redeemers."

Ruth 2:20

Naomi is excited about the fact that Boaz, as their kinsman-redeemer, can **rescue** them from their poverty! As we continue our study, we'll soon see Boaz redeeming Ruth from her dire situation. Jesus Christ was and is our kinsman-redeemer. He redeems us from the bondage of **sin**.

God didn't have to redeem us. God wasn't obligated to save us, and we certainly don't deserve to be redeemed. So why do you think God chose to offer us salvation?

_____

_____

_____

_____

_____

_____

Let's take a peek at one of the most well-known verses in the Bible—John 3:16. According to this passage, what is God's method of redeeming us? (What or whom did God use to offer us salvation?)

_____

_____

_____

_____

Then Ruth the Moabite said, "He even said to me, 'Stay with my workers until they finish harvesting all my grain.'"

Naomi said to Ruth her daughter-in-law, "It will be good for you, my daughter, to go with the women who work for him, because in someone else's field you might be harmed."

Ruth 2:21–22

Harvest time was a great celebration! Think *party* in the best sense of the word! There would be lots of young men and women present at the harvest celebration. Ruth could easily be swayed to look to a younger man for **romantic** interest. But she's a woman of God and a woman of character. No doubt she feels God's hand on her friendship with Boaz, though she still doesn't have the full picture of what will happen with this **romance**. She's not yet able to see what God has in store for her. But she continues to **trust** God's plan.

Ruth also trusts her mother-in-law. She has watched

Naomi live out her **faith** during the lean years of poverty and grief in Moab. She knows Naomi has a deep, growing, **intimate** relationship with God.

What do those around you know about your relationship with God? Do you keep it private? Do you talk openly about God? Are you seen as a young woman of faith? Or a young woman of obedience? Or a young woman of uncertainty?

_____

_____

_____

_____

> So Ruth stayed close to the women of Boaz to glean until the barley and wheat harvests were finished. And she lived with her mother-in-law.
>
> Ruth 2:23

Just as Ruth **heeds** the advice of her mother-in-law, we too need to heed the advice of older, spiritually mature adults in our lives. Too often we look past an elderly person and his or her advice simply because of age. The truth is that many older people in our churches today are **saints**! They've lived through the lean times and can strongly testify to God's provision. God **often** chooses to speak through wise adults. If we'd learn to seek them out and listen to them, we'd gain valuable spiritual **insights**.

Think of an older, spiritually mature person whom you respect and can look to for spiritual guidance. Write his or her name here:

_____

_____

_____

Letter of Encouragement

Will you jot this person a note of **encouragement** right now? Let him or her know of your respect and admiration. Ask for prayer from this person and look forward to what God will **teach** you through this life.

_____

_____

_____

_____

_____

_____

_____

_____

BITE #8

GRAB A FRIEND

You did it! You just finished the second chapter of Ruth. You're a Secret Power Girl who is growing closer to Christ because you're taking his Word seriously. Now grab a friend and discuss the following questions together, or write your ideas in the journal pages.

- Describe what a kinsman-redeemer is.

- Boaz blessed the gleaners in his field. How have I blessed people in my life this past week?

- Boaz affirms Ruth for taking refuge under the wings of God. Was there a time this week when I sought refuge from a person other than God?

- Ruth is a woman of character. How has my character been revealed this week?

Memorize It!

Try to memorize this verse with your friend and say it to each other the next time you get together.

"May you be richly rewarded by the LORD, the God of Israel, under whose wings you have come to take refuge."

Ruth 2:12

My Journal

Okay S.P.G., this is your space, so take advantage of it. You can do whatever you want here, but always try to include the following:

@ List your prayer requests. (Later, as God answers them, go back and record the date when God answered your prayer.)

@ Copy down any verse we studied in the previous chapter that you don't understand. Then let this be a reminder to ask your parents, Sunday school teacher, pastor, or youth leader about it.

@ Jot down what stood out the most from this chapter.

SECTION THREE

Girl Visits Guy

Ruth 3:1–18

BITE #1

Before we dive into Scripture, let's take a moment to recap. It's been established that **Boaz** is Naomi's relative. Therefore, he's also Ruth's relative. He is her **kinsman-redeemer**. He can save her from her poverty and fill the void in her life that her husband left when he died.

We've looked at a couple of interesting **laws** thus far in the book of Ruth, haven't we? The law that provided food for the poor by allowing them to glean after the harvesters and the kinsman-redeemer law.

To understand the rest of the romance that unfolds in the book of Ruth, we need to take a look at another strange law. It's found in Deuteronomy 25:5–10:

> If brothers are living together and one of them dies without a son, his widow must not marry outside the family. Her husband's brother shall take her and marry her and fulfill the duty of a brother-in-law to her. The first son she bears shall carry on the name of the dead brother so that his name will not be blotted out from Israel.
>
> However, if a man does not want to marry his brother's wife, she shall go to the elders at the town gate and say, "My husband's brother refuses to carry on his brother's name in Israel. He will not fulfill the duty of a brother-in-law to me." Then the elders of his town shall summon him and talk to him. If he persists in saying, "I do not want to marry her," his brother's widow shall go up to him in the presence of the elders, take off one of his sandals, spit in his face and say, "This is what is done to the man who will not build up his brother's family line." That man's line shall be known in Israel as The Family of the Unsandaled.

Wingclips

While it's tempting to **laugh** at this strange law, it did have a positive spin to it. In those days this law bonded families **together**. Every family member was extremely interested and involved in the girl each son would marry. **Brothers** were especially interested because they could end up having to marry the woman if their brother died.

Just as we saw how the gleaning law was God's **provision** for the poor, we can see two more examples of God's provision in this law.

One: *God wanted to protect women.* Think about it: Back then women without husbands didn't have the legal right to own land. So if a woman's husband died, and she was left with a farm, cattle, sheep, or a vineyard, she'd be up a creek without a paddle—because she had very little legal defense if someone else laid claim to her property. God's law allowed her to claim help immediately through a brother of her husband or the nearest guardian.

No doubt you've heard many times, "God loves you. God loves everybody." But to know that God is specifically interested in taking care of women should make you feel pretty good!

Circle all the words that describe how you feel knowing God has a special interest in you as a young woman.

ticked off   alone

expectant   stubborn   Happy

secure

loved   disrespectful   pressured

confident   comforted

excited   old   special

inadequate   confused   respected

cherished   provided for

prideful   disobedient

Two: *God wanted to protect land rights.* Earlier in our study of Ruth, we learned how God had promised the Israelites land. (It's referred to as the Promised Land.) And not only did God provide land for the nation of Israel, but he also gave each tribe a specific portion of land and each family within the tribe a certain piece of land as well.

But we also learned that a family could lose its land. If you'll flip back to BITE #2 in chapter two, you'll recall the example of Mr. Smith. He owns forty acres of land, but his crops haven't produced, so he sells his land to Mr. Jones (who can only purchase the mortgage for up to fifty years; after that time the land will go back to the Smith family).

Okay, we understand that. It was God's way of keeping the land in the family. But now we see God going a step further to protect land rights. What if a widow married a stranger? He'd have automatic rights to her property. This law (that the widow had to marry within the family of her deceased husband) was God's way of protecting the land for the people.

The Bible makes it extremely clear that God is interested in *every* one of our needs!

Mark the following statements true or false.

It's easy for me to give my needs to God.

_____ True _____ False

I've seen God meet my needs.

_____ True _____ False

I know God wants me to trust him with everything I need.

_____ True _____ False

It's easier for me to believe God cares about the big needs in my life than about the smaller needs I have.

_____ True _____ False

It's easier for me to believe God cares about the small needs in my life than about the bigger needs I have.

_____ True _____ False

It's hard for me to truly believe that God cares about every one of my needs.

_____ True _____ False

If you're having a tough time believing that God really cares about meeting your needs, take a moment to list the needs you've had and how God has provided.

_____

_____

_____

Grab your Bible and turn to 1 Peter 5:7. What are you told to do?

Be content

_____

_____

What **reason** are you given for doing this?

promote at the right time

_____

_____

Now turn to Ephesians 5:29. What is Christ's love for the church compared to in this verse?

husband's love

_____

_____

Who God is

Check out Psalm 111:5. For whom does God provide food? And how long will God remember this covenant?

to those who fear Him

Forever

Let's look at 1 Timothy 6:17. What does God provide for us?

piles on riches

Question to Ponder

Take a moment to write a text message of thanksgiving for God's provision. Strive to list specific things God has provided for you. Try not to write a "general" message. Really think about what you can thank God for!

BITE #2

> One day Ruth's mother-in-law Naomi said to her, "My daughter, I must find a home for you, where you will be well provided for. Now Boaz, with whose women you have worked, is a relative of ours."
>
> Ruth 3:1–2

Now we come to an interesting twist in this beautiful romance. Ruth knows Boaz is a kinsman-redeemer of hers. He's the one who can step in and provide for her. She knows he's interested in her. He's given quite a few signals. Think of the **signs** Boaz has given Ruth to let her know he's personally interested in her.

So why doesn't Boaz go ahead and make his move? you may be thinking. *She knows he's interested. Why doesn't he ask her out?*

We're led to believe that he'd **love** to do that right now, but his hands are tied! Boaz has to wait for Ruth to do the claiming! She has to **claim** him as her kinsman-redeemer.

We've discussed how Boaz—as Ruth's kinsman-redeemer—is parallel to Christ being *our* kinsman-redeemer. Now think about another similarity: just as Ruth has to claim Boaz, you, too, have to claim Christ as your **Savior**.

Boaz can't force Ruth to claim him. And Jesus won't **force** you to accept him either!

wow

How does this make you feel about Boaz? About God? About Ruth?

_____

_____

_____

Ruth hasn't made her move. So we read that her mother-in-law finally speaks out. Let's take another look at the Scripture:

> One day Ruth's mother-in-law Naomi said to her, "My daughter, I must find a home for you, where you will be well provided for. Now Boaz, with whose women you have worked, is a relative of ours."
>
> Ruth 3:1–2

Naomi gently **encourages** Ruth to move forward. But we need to understand that Naomi isn't being pushy; she's simply nudging Ruth in the direction **God** wants her to head. We also need to understand that although Ruth is **moving** forward, she's not _being_ forward.

Describe the difference between being forward and moving forward.

_____

_____

_____

Girls often **mistakenly** can be too forward in letting a guy know she likes him. *There's nothing wrong with asking a guy out,* she thinks. *And he's so shy! If I don't make a move, nothing will ever happen. So I **have** to make the first move!*

Whoa! Slow down, girlfriend. It's time for a reminder: it's a *wise* young woman who will allow God to direct her dating relationships. The gal who feels she has to control things herself is a gal who's not allowing God to be in total control of her life.

How can a girl's actions demonstrate that she doesn't fully trust God when she tries to initiate a relationship?

_____

_____

_____

Read the following two scenarios and notice the distinction.

"I've liked Todd forever," Emily tells Beth. *"We're good friends, but I wonder if anything will ever develop beyond that."*

"Does he know you'd like to become more than friends?" Beth asks.

"I don't know," Emily replies.

"Well, maybe you'd better tell him."

"Ah, I don't know."

"Go ahead, Emily. Just tell him how you feel. You've gotta find out if he likes you back!"

"Okay, Beth. I think I'll write him a note."

"You go, girl!"

"I'm kinda nervous."

"Well . . . it's a risk to let him know your feelings. But you have to do it, Em! If you don't, you may never know how he feels."

"What if he doesn't feel the same way?"

"You'll never know till you write the note!"

"I just feel kinda weird. I wish he'd just make a move; you know—tell me how he feels—give me a signal, something."

"Yeah, well . . . not gonna happen," Beth says. "Write the note."

"Okay. I'll do it," Emily says.

* * *

"Hi, Emily! How's it going?" Beth asks.

"Whew, I'm tired," Emily says. "Todd and I have been working on our science project for the past two hours."

"You guys sure are good friends, huh?"

Emily laughs. "We really are. We've known each other since kindergarten."

"Wow! That's forever," Beth says. "Have your feelings ever gone beyond friendship?"

"Yeah, I've been crushing on him for the past two years."

"Seriously? Does he know?"

"If he does, he's never said anything."

"And you've never told him?" Beth asks.

"Nope."

"Girl, you've gotta let him know! If he knew how you felt, you two might be a serious couple right now," Beth says.

"Yeah, I've thought about that," Emily says. "Todd's everything I want in a guy. He's a strong Christian, and he cares about others. I really like him."

"Ooooh, girl! This is gettin' good! So write him a note!"

"Nah," Emily says. "I've been praying about it, and I just don't feel it's what God wants me to do."

"Okay, what language are you talkin'?"

Emily laughs again. "Think about it, Beth. Todd's a smart guy. He's certainly intelligent enough to know that I like him. If he wants to act on that, great! If not, I'll keep being his friend."

"I can't believe this," Beth says. "He's so shy! He's probably scared to say anything—thinking he'll ruin the friendship or something. You've gotta tell him!"

"Not gonna do it. About a year ago, I put my dating life in God's control."

"So? What's that supposed to mean?"

"It means that I believe if it's God's will for Todd

and me to become more than friends, God will make it happen."

"Okay," Beth continues. "But what if you don't see God move? What if Todd doesn't say or do anything to place your friendship into the romance category? Then what?"

"I'll keep trusting God. If nothing more than friendship happens with Todd, I believe God has someone else in mind for me."

"Yeah, but Em! Don't you wanna know how Todd feels about you?"

"Sure! I'd love to know. But get this, Beth. If I write him a note or talk to him and tell him my feelings for him go deeper than friendship, he'll either return my feelings and tell me he likes me as more than a friend, too—"

"Yeah! So go for it, Em!"

"Or," Emily continues, "he'll gently let me know that he doesn't feel the same way. That could damage our friendship. Things would be really awkward."

"Love is worth taking the risk. I still say let him know!"

"Hold on, Beth. Even if I tell him my feelings and he returns them, I'll always wonder if he ever would've taken the initiative to make the first move. I've learned I'm valuable in God's eyes, Beth—so valuable that I don't have to take my love life into my own hands. If a guy wants to pursue me, he has to take the first step.

I'm worth that."

"Hmmm. I like that," Beth says. "I wanna feel that valuable too. So often I just get ahead of myself and blurt out how I feel. But you know something? I'm worth having a guy approach me too!"

"You're exactly right, Beth. And when you totally surrender your dating life to God's control, it takes all the pressure off of you. You don't have to think, 'How can I get him to notice me? Does he like me? How can I get his attention?' You can just relax and be friends with the guy and trust that God is big enough to make something more happen if it's God's will."

Do you understand the **difference** between truly surrendering your relationships to God and trying to make something happen yourself?

You may be thinking, *the Bible just told Ruth to make her move.*

Remember the law. In those days a widow had to **claim** her kinsman-redeemer. Ruth didn't move to Bethlehem and start chasing guys. Her **priorities** are right. She's **focused** on God and on taking care of her mother-in-law.

Allowing God to be in charge of your dating life doesn't mean you'll never speak to **guys**. God wants you to be friendly, reach out, and make those around you comfortable. Guys will naturally gravitate to girls with whom they're **comfortable**. So learning the art of being a good conversationalist, showing genuine interest

in the guy you like, and developing a good friendship are
wise choices.

But you can do the above **without** chasing a guy. God
created **males** to be the pursuers. And guess what! **You're
definitely worth being pursued!**

Prayer to Ponder

**Take a moment to create a pledge allowing God to be in
charge of your relationships.**

_____

_____

_____

_____

_____

_____

_____

_____

_____

_____

BITE #3

"Tonight he will be winnowing barley on the threshing floor. Wash, put on perfume, and get dressed in your best clothes. Then go down to the threshing floor, but don't let him know you are there until he has finished eating and drinking. When he lies down, note the place where he is lying. Then go and uncover his feet and lie down. He will tell you what to do."

"I will do whatever you say," Ruth answered.

Ruth 3:2–5

Naomi tells Ruth to get **dressed up**. You can imagine that she uses her best bath oils and her favorite perfume and puts on the nicest outfit she has. There's nothing wrong with wanting to **look good**. When we take **care** of ourselves, we usually **feel** better about ourselves. In today's culture, she would've had her hair done, gotten a manicure and pedicure, and showered with Bath & Body Works gel, then used fragrant lotion and body spray.

Sometimes people think Christians shouldn't be concerned with their appearance. Though we're told in Proverbs 31:30 and in 1 Peter 3:3–4 that outer beauty is fleeting and true beauty comes from the inside, we shouldn't use this as an excuse to let ourselves go. It makes sense to want to look our best, plus makeovers are fun! It only becomes wrong when we become obsessed with our looks.

Look up
Ruth movie?
Threshing floor

Ruth does what Naomi tells her. She bathes, dresses, and heads to the threshing floor. It may seem as though Ruth is being forward. But again we have to understand the culture and what the threshing floor was. So pretend you're stepping back in history a few thousand years. Here's the scene: The threshing floor is a smooth **surface**. It's more than likely clay soil that's been packed and hardened. It's marked off with rocks in a circular area.

Most threshing floors are at the top of a **hill**, so pretend you're up high. About midafternoon you begin to feel a **breeze**. The threshing will continue as long as there's a breeze. If you look closely, you'll notice sheaves of grain all over the floor. **Watch out!** Here come the oxen. Don't get in their way. They're **trampling** the grain that's spread all over the floor.

The oxen aren't the only ones working. The threshing floor is filled with people wildly **throwing** the grain up into the air. The chaff is blown away by the breeze, and the **good grain** comes down on the threshing floor.

The threshing won't stop until the **wind** dies down. That might be 5:00 p.m. or it could be midnight. At that point you're going to party! Actually, it's a religious feast, a huge **celebration**. After you've had your fill, you'll join the **families** and the rest of the folks on the threshing floor to catch a few zzzz's. And you're glad because you've worked hard and you're dog tired!

The threshing floor is **circular**. The men are sleeping with their heads toward the grain, and their **feet** are sticking out like bicycle spokes. *How come they're sleeping this way?* you may be thinking.

It's to **protect** the grain from thieves. If someone comes in to steal the grain (he'd have to be pretty brave—or stupid—to try to force his way through all the men lying in the circle), he'll have to walk toward the men to get the grain. Each man in the circle, because of this sleeping position, will find it easier to jump up and face the thief. In other words, the robber **will have** to come toward the men; it's impossible for him to sneak around them or creep up behind them.

> So she went down to the threshing floor and did everything her mother-in-law told her to do.
>
> Ruth 3:6

Ruth doesn't question Naomi because she **trusts** her mother-in-law's relationship with God. Ruth knows God is leading Naomi to guide her in this way.

Think of the people in your life who are in authority over you (parents, teachers, youth leaders, pastors, etc.). Choose two people and identify what makes it easy for you to trust them.

1. _____

2. _____

Do you have difficulty trusting certain people in authority over you? If so, why?

_____

_____

_____

Think about Ruth's past several **weeks**. She's been gleaning in the field. She's been _taking_ grain. Now she's on the threshing floor for a higher **purpose**.

Now think about yourself for a moment. Maybe you've been gleaning and taking. **That's good**. We all need to glean; we all need to take and receive. But there comes a point in our spiritual lives when we need to stop taking all the time and start **giving**.

God has a high calling on your life! And God wants you to glean and take spiritual food—all you can get! But God also wants you to **give**.

During the past two weeks of your life, have you been doing more taking than giving? What have you spiritually taken, and what have you spiritually given?

_____

_____

_____

_____

The Secret Power of **LOVE**

> When Boaz had finished eating and drinking and was in good spirits, he went over to lie down at the far end of the grain pile. Ruth approached quietly, uncovered his feet and lay down. In the middle of the night something startled the man; he turned—and there was a woman lying at his feet!
>
> Ruth 3:7–8

Let's make sure we're on the **right page** with Ruth. Again, she's not being forward **or** improper. Naomi would **never** have suggested that her daughter-in-law do something immoral. The threshing floor is a **public** place. Ruth isn't going to bed with Boaz. She *is* going near him, but it's for a specific **purpose**: to claim him as her kinsman-redeemer.

Ruth is lying at the **feet** of Boaz, and she has pulled the covers away from his feet. The Scripture tells us, "In the middle of the night something startled the man." He may have heard an animal; someone may have thrown an extra log on the fire; or it could have been any number of noises. **But he wakes up.**

Identify a time when something startled you in the middle of the night. Perhaps it was a dream, a person, or a thunderstorm.

_____

_____

_____

145

Have your fears at night changed from when you were a child?

_____

_____

_____

_____

When you're afraid, Christ wants you to turn to him. He cares about everything that concerns you! Grab your Bible and turn to Deuteronomy 1:21. What are we told not to do?

_____

_____

_____

_____

Now look at Hebrews 13:6. Who wants to be our helper during scary times?

_____

_____

_____

_____

Read John 14:27. Insert your own name into this verse and rewrite it in your own words in the space provided.

_____

_____

_____

_____

_____

_____

_____

_____

_____

_____

_____

_____

_____

_____

_____

_____

_____

BITE #4

"Who are you?" he asked.

"I am your servant Ruth," she said. "Spread the corner of your garment over me, since you are a kinsman-redeemer of our family."

Ruth 3:9

Something startles Boaz, and he wakes up. Now that he's awake, he realizes his feet are **cold**. But when he reaches for the blanket at his feet, he notices a woman. He probably squints his eyes and tries to adjust his sight to the darkness of the night.

Ruth identifies herself.

To identify yourself, you have to know who you are. You may feel as though you're right in the middle of **discovering** who you really are. It can be a **process**. Know that **true identity** is found in a strong, growing, intimate relationship with your Creator.

The more you get to know the One who made you . . .

_____ a. the wealthier you'll become.

_____ b. the more you'll understand who you are.

_____ c. the more you'll enjoy fishing.

_____ d. the more you'll travel.

Questions to Ponder

Besides discovering your own identity, you'll need to discover another identity in life. Every person in the world (you included!) has to decide who Jesus is. Do you know the identity of Christ? Do you truly understand who he is?

_____

_____

_____

Who _is_ Jesus Christ?

_____ a. A good teacher

_____ b. A prophet

_____ c. A wise man

_____ d. The Messiah, Son of God, King of Kings

John the Baptist, the cousin of Jesus, asked about Christ's identity. Check out Matthew 11:2–3. What question does John send his disciples to ask Jesus?

_____

_____

_____

And according to Matthew 11:4–6, what is Jesus's response?

_____

_____

_____

Jesus won't force you to believe that he's the Son of God. But for all who believe, he forgives sins and grants eternal life! Describe the time when you accepted Jesus Christ as the Son of God and asked him to become your Savior.

_____

_____

_____

_____

Back to Ruth. When she went to the threshing floor, where did she lie?

_____ a. On a water bed

_____ b. On a hammock

_____ c. On a tanning bed

_____ d. At the feet of Boaz

Thus far in our study of Ruth, we've seen some parallels between Boaz and Christ. Circle all the similarities.

Boaz & Jesus provided for the poor. Jesus & Boaz both had disciples. Jesus & Boaz never forced people to love them. Boaz & Jesus both loved grain sandwiches. Boaz & Jesus ate a unique grain cereal for breakfast every morning of their lives. Boaz is Ruth's kinsman-redeemer, and Christ is our kinsman-redeemer. Jesus & Boaz both wore Doc Martens sandals. Jesus & Boaz were kind to all.

Ruth lies at the **feet** of Boaz. Let's take a quick peek at the **feet** of Jesus. He's Ruler of the **calm** as he walks on the seashore. He's Lord of the **storm** as he walks on the water's waves. Imagine his **feet** being nailed to the cross for you. These are the same **feet** that left the glory and splendor of heaven to invade your world with **love**. These **feet** were born in a crude, dirty stable. Yet these same feet **walked** to the tomb of Lazarus and raised him from the dead. These are the feet that walked in the **temple** and the feet that walked up Mount Calvary for *you.*

According to John 1:36, what does John the Baptist say when he sees Jesus walking?

_____

_____

_____

_____

Where have the feet of Jesus led you this week as you've walked with him?

_____

_____

_____

_____

BITE #5

Before we dive into further Scripture, let's review a few past verses:

> When Boaz had finished eating and drinking and was in good spirits, he went over to lie down at the far end of the grain pile. Ruth approached quietly, uncovered his feet and lay down. In the middle of the night something startled the man; he turned—and there was a woman lying at his feet!
>
> "Who are you?" he asked.
>
> "I am your servant Ruth," she said. "Spread the corner of your garment over me, since you are a kinsman-redeemer of our family."
>
> Ruth 3:7–9

Remember that Ruth isn't doing something immoral or immodest in lying at the feet of Boaz. Her actions show Boaz that she wants him to be a **spiritual covering** for her. She's asking him to become her kinsman-redeemer.

Create some dialogue between Ruth and Boaz in today's language that will explain what she's asking.

_____

_____

_____

_____

Ruth sees Boaz as her only hope. As far as she knows, he's her only kinsman-redeemer. He's the only one who can step in and save her, help her, and provide for her. Identify a time in your life when your back was against a wall and you realized that Jesus was your only hope.

_____

_____

_____

The question now is: **Will Boaz do it?** Will this well-to-do rich man stretch his garment to cover a *poor* Moabite woman who has no money and nothing to offer? Will he do it?

Maybe you're at the **same** point in life. Perhaps you're wondering if God's blanket of forgiveness can actually reach **you**. Can it truly cover **all** your sins? Not only can God's **forgiveness** cover all your sins, but God's **grace** also completely erases your sins!

Grab your **Bible** and turn to Psalm 103:11. According to this passage, how much does God love you?

_____

_____

_____

Now read Psalm 103:12. How far have your sins been removed from God's mind?

_____

_____

_____

Imagine! God chooses to forget your sins! When you ask Jesus for forgiveness, he completely wipes your record clean! You're brand-new—without stain. How does this make you feel? (Mark all that apply.)

_____ a. Like jumping up and down on a trampoline forever!

_____ b. Giggly, gracious, giddy, grateful!

_____ c. Like I wanna run into Jesus's arms and thank him for about 10,000 years without stopping!

_____ d. Peaceful, pure, purposeful, polished, pleased, positive!

_____ e. Like drinking a tall, cold glass of lemonade and letting it spill down my chin!

_____ f. Hugs, hallelujah, hopeful, hosanna!

_____ g. Like I wanna live my whole life for Christ in thanks for what he's done for me!

_____ h. Forgiven, fanciful, free!

_____ i. Other _____

Christ is your **Redeemer**! This is a word that indicates a **continued** state of action. In other words, Christ didn't simply redeem you one time when you gave your life to him and that was it. He will continually, **consistently**, constantly cover you with his garment, forgive you, and provide for you no matter how long you've lived in Moab—the garbage dump.

God will always forgive a **repentant** heart. God will continue to redeem **genuine** confession. But genuine repentance doesn't say, "Tonight I'll ask God to forgive me for shoplifting this lipstick. But tomorrow if I don't have enough money to buy that CD I want, I'll probably just grab it and ask God to forgive me later. Then next week I may go shopping and take a pair of jeans. I'll just ask God to forgive me again. And when it's time for prom, I'll probably lift some new shoes. God will forgive me."

That's *not* genuine repentance!

Genuine repentance says, "Oh, dear Lord. I'm so sorry I sinned. Will you forgive me? I realize that by sinning, I've broken your heart. I'm so sorry. I don't ever plan on going that direction again. In fact, I'm going to set up some accountability and safeguards in my life that will help me stay away from this area of sin. I'm so sorry."

As seen in *The Secret Power of Grace,* a Bible study book on 1 Peter, when we've totally surrendered every area in our lives to Christ, and when we yield to the authority of his Holy Spirit in our lives, we don't have to continue living as **slaves** to sin. God wants to **free** us from being enslaved to sin.

Look at what the apostle John says in 1 John 2:1:

My dear children, I write this to you so that you will not sin.

John wouldn't have told us not to sin if it weren't **possible**! We're not puppets! We don't have to be **controlled** by our sinful desires. With God's Holy Spirit ruling, **empowering**, and saturating our lives, we **can** say no to temptation!

But we're still human. There may be times when we don't say no, and we **do** sin. If that happens, what will we do? We can find the answer in 1 John 2:1:

But if anybody does sin, we have an advocate with the Father—Jesus Christ, the Righteous One.

That's proof that God will always forgive a genuinely repentant heart! Christ will **continue to redeem** us when we come to him and offer confession.

Susie Shellenberger

Prayer to Ponder

Take a moment to ask God if there is any unconfessed sin in your life right now for which you need to seek forgiveness. Use Psalm 139:23–24 as your prayer guide.

BITE #6

> "The LORD bless you, my daughter," he replied. "This kindness is greater than that which you showed earlier: You have not run after the younger men, whether rich or poor."
>
> Ruth 3:10

We **quickly** realize from this passage that Boaz is willing to be Ruth's kinsman-redeemer. He has been impressed with Ruth. He has watched her and admired her lifestyle. It's as if he's saying, "I noticed you didn't move here and simply start chasing guys. You focused entirely on God. You're not flippant. You haven't let the young, good-looking guys distract you. You've kept your focus. I like that. You have tons of character. You're trustworthy."

> "And now, my daughter, don't be afraid. I will do for you all you ask. All the people of my town know that you are a woman of noble character."
>
> Ruth 3:11

Yes! Not only is Boaz *willing* to be her kinsman-redeemer—but he also *wants* to be her kinsman-redeemer. He has been eagerly waiting for her to claim him.

Susie Shellenberger

Again, how does this parallel with Christ wanting to be your Redeemer?

_____

_____

_____

_____

_____

Let's take another look at Boaz's last sentence in this passage:

> "All the people of my town know that you are a woman of noble character."
>
> Ruth 3:11

Ruth's reputation has gotten around town. Everyone knows she's a woman of integrity. They admire her. What would the people of your town say about you?

Finish this sentence about yourself: "All the other students know that I am a woman of _____."

Let's take another look at Ruth 3:10:

> "The Lord bless you, my daughter," he replied. "This kindness is greater than that which you showed earlier: You have not run after the younger men, whether rich or poor."

162

The fact that Ruth has chosen to glean in the field of Boaz . . .

_____ a. ticks him off.

_____ b. makes him laugh.

_____ c. makes him happy.

_____ d. confuses him.

Boaz takes it as a compliment that Ruth has selected his field instead of another. Can you imagine how happy Jesus is and was when you answered his call to come to him? Try to imagine your Redeemer saying this to you: "I know there are tons of **religions** talked about today. I chose you to be on my team a long time ago, but you had to accept. You also had to choose me. And I'm so happy you've chosen **Christianity**. It's the only true faith! I am the absolute **only** way you'll ever get to heaven. And you've made the right choice! I'm so **glad** you're serving the one true God!"

Do you know that when you make wise choices, when you give God praise, and when you focus on God, you're actually **blessing** God?

Imagine your Redeemer saying this to you: "You have lots of choices on Sunday morning, but you've chosen to be in my house with my people. That blesses me. You had other options: you could have slept in, gone shopping, spent two hours on Facebook, or watched TV. But you're where you need to be, and you're lifting your voice in praise to me—I'm blessed by that."

Not only is Boaz willing, but he's also excited to be Ruth's kinsman-redeemer. The love story is unfolding, isn't it?

How do you view your relationship with your Savior? (Mark all that apply.)

I don't have a relationship with Him.

Jesus is not only my savior, but he's also my best friend.

I don't know.

It's an obligation.

I have a lot of doubts.

I'm so happy I'm serving Jesus.

It's a love relationship.

My relationship with Christ is based on fear.

I delight in my relationship with Christ.

talk to one of us after

Christ **passionately** loves you. He willingly **died** for you! One of the most exciting things about Christianity is that we can enjoy a warm, loving, personal relationship with the Creator of the universe!

How has your lifestyle reflected this in the past week?

_____

_____

_____

Question to Ponder

Write down what you can imagine your Redeemer saying to you as you read, study, and memorize Scripture.

_____

_____

_____

_____

_____

_____

_____

_____

BITE #7

"Although it is true that I am a kinsman-redeemer of our family, there is another who is more closely related than I. Stay here for the night, and in the morning if he wants to do his duty as your kinsman-redeemer, good; let him redeem you. But if he is not willing, as surely as the Lord lives I will do it. Lie here until morning."

Ruth 3:12–13

What?! Now we find out that Boaz actually isn't the closest living relative to Naomi and Ruth. How does Boaz know that? We can assume that he's so eager to become Ruth's kinsman-redeemer that he's **checked** around to see if he actually is the next in line. But in his search, he discovered that there's another man who actually is more closely related to her than himself.

Boaz doesn't send Ruth home. He **protects** her by not letting her out on the dark streets of Bethlehem at night. He's **concerned** for her safety. Your Redeemer also wants to protect and comfort **you**.

Describe a time in your life when you felt protected or comforted by your Redeemer.

_____

_____

_____

Susie Shellenberger

Grab your Bible and read Psalm 41:2. What promise do you find?

_____

_____

_____

Check out Psalm 91:14. Why will God protect you?

_____

_____

_____

Look at 2 Corinthians 1:3–4. Who will comfort you in all your troubles?

_____

_____

_____

Why will God comfort you?

_____

_____

_____

According to Jeremiah 31:13, what does God want to give you?

_____

_____

_____

Boaz also **comforts** Ruth by telling her, "Lie down; go to sleep; don't worry about it; I'll take care of things." When **you're** faced with uncertainty, Jesus wants you to trust him and let him take care of your problems. Let's look at Proverbs 3:5–6:

> "Trust in the Lord with all your heart and lean not on your own understanding; in all your ways submit to him, and he will make your paths straight."

According to this passage, what should you do in trying times?

_____

_____

_____

And what benefit will you reap if you trust God?

_____

_____

_____

Susie Shellenberger

Grab your Bible and flip to Proverbs 22:19. Whom should you trust?

_____

_____

_____

Now flip to Isaiah 8:17. What two things are you encouraged to do?

_____

_____

_____

_____

Take a peek at Isaiah 12:2:

"Surely God is my salvation; I will trust and not be afraid. The Lord, the Lord himself, is my strength and my defense; he has become my salvation."

What three things does God want to be for you, according to the above verse?

1. _____

2. _____

3. _____

What does God tell you to do instead of being afraid?

_____

_____

_____

Now turn to Isaiah 26:4. How long should you trust in the Lord?

_____

_____

_____

What is the Lord compared to in this passage?

_____

_____

_____

In what areas of your life do you have the most difficulty trusting God?

_____

_____

_____

Susie Shellenberger

Prayer to Ponder

Write out a prayer, placing these areas in God's care.

_____

_____

_____

_____

_____

_____

_____

_____

_____

_____

_____

_____

_____

_____

_____

BITE #8

So she lay at his feet until morning, but got up before anyone could be recognized; and he said, "No one must know that a woman came to the threshing floor."

Ruth 3:14

Boaz knows another man is more closely **related** to Ruth and Naomi. He wants Ruth to leave the threshing floor before anyone else can see her, in case the other relative has any interest in her. If the other man is interested in becoming Ruth's kinsman-redeemer and knows Boaz is also interested, he may quickly exclude Boaz. Boaz wants to handle this **himself**.

He also said, "Bring me the shawl you are wearing and hold it out." When she did so, he poured into it six measures of barley and placed the bundle on her. Then he went back to town.

Ruth 3:15

Boaz gives Ruth an extremely generous gift, doesn't he? Note how many measures of barley he gives her.

This is interesting. We're told in Genesis that God created the world in six days. God worked for six and rested on the seventh after the work was complete.

Perhaps Boaz is sending a message to Naomi through Ruth. "Don't worry, I'll work at this. I'll work hard at it, and I won't rest until my work is completed—until Ruth is my wife."

If this **is** a message from Boaz, it goes right over Ruth's head. But remember, she's still a **young** believer. Her faith is still growing. She hasn't walked with the Lord as long as her **mother-in-law** has.

But even if **Ruth** doesn't get the tricky message, we're led to believe in verse 18 that Naomi **understands**.

> When Ruth came to her mother-in-law, Naomi asked, "How did it go, my daughter?"
>
> Then she told her everything Boaz had done for her and added, "He gave me these six measures of barley, saying, 'Don't go back to your mother-in-law empty-handed.'"
>
> Then Naomi said, "Wait, my daughter, until you find out what happens. For the man will not rest until the matter is settled today."
>
> Ruth 3:16–18

In other words, "Ruth, you can relax now. Sit back and wait. Boaz will work it all out. In fact, he's a man on a mission! He won't even stop to rest until he's accomplished his goal."

Your purpose as a young woman is **not** to go out and make something happen with a guy. **Wait.** Let God and the guy work it out!

In what areas of your life do you find it most difficult to wait on God's timing?

_____

_____

_____

_____

_____

_____

Ruth rests. She's done all she can do. She's claimed Boaz as her redeemer; now he'll do the rest.

When we come to Christ, we come in faith. All he asks is that we confess our sins, accept his gift of forgiveness, and live for him. He **doesn't** ask us to pay for our sins. He **doesn't** suggest that we try to "work it all out" or earn our salvation. **We can't.** We just have to surrender, rest, and let him do his wonderful work within us.

And the exciting part? He's given us a **promise** concerning the work that he's doing inside us. Read Philippians 1:6 and jot down what is said about the work God is doing inside **you**.

BITE #9

GRAB A FRIEND

Yahoo! You just finished the third chapter of Ruth. Now grab a friend and discuss the following questions together.

@ Am I demonstrating that God is in control of my dating life and that I fully trust God? Or have I taken control and tried to make things happen with a guy this week?

@ Is there anything in my lifestyle that's immodest in my relationship with guys? (Examples: the way I dress, the way I act, etc.)

@ How have I blessed God this week?

@ Describe a specific time this week that you turned to God for comfort and protection during uncertain times.

Memorize It!

Try to memorize this verse with your friend and say it to each other the next time you get together.

"All the people of my town know that you are a woman of noble character."

Ruth 3:11

My Journal

Okay, S.P.G., this is your space, so take advantage of it. You can do whatever you want here, but always try to include the following:

@ List your prayer requests. (Later, as God answers them, go back and record the date when God answered your prayer.)

@ Copy down any verse we studied in the previous chapter that you don't understand. Then let this be a reminder to ask your parents, Sunday school teacher, pastor, or youth leader about it.

@ Jot down what stood out the most from this chapter.

Girl Gets Guy

Ruth 4:1–22

BITE #1

Meanwhile Boaz went up to the town gate and sat down there just as the kinsman-redeemer he had mentioned came along.

Ruth 4:1

Where does Boaz go?

_____ a. He goes to the courthouse.

_____ b. He goes to the city gate.

_____ c. He goes to the place where business transactions occur.

Boaz actually goes to all of the above. The town gate served as a sort of courthouse in those days. It was the **place** where all business transactions happened.

Why does Boaz go to the town gate?

_____ a. He wants to climb over the gate and escape.

_____ b. He wants to take the other guardian to court.

_____ c. He knows the guardian will have to enter through the gate at some time during the day.

_____ d. He's planning to kill the other relative at the courthouse.

Boaz knows that the other relative will **eventually** have to walk through the gate, so he waits there for him. Boaz wants to act quickly and make himself Ruth's legal kinsman-redeemer, so he will meet the man at the gate and take him to court.

Boaz is certainly going out of his way for Ruth, isn't he? Describe how Christ went out of his way for you.

_____

_____

_____

_____

Identify a time when _you_ went out of your way for someone you loved.

_____

_____

_____

Boaz said, "Come over here, my friend, and sit down." So he went over and sat down.

Ruth 4:1

We don't know the exact **relation** of this other man to Naomi. In those days you were a relative or you weren't. People weren't referred to as a **second cousin** or a cousin once removed. You were related or you weren't.

This other man may be a **brother** of Naomi's deceased husband, Elimelek. Perhaps Boaz is simply a **cousin**. They probably know each other because they're related and both lived and worked in **Bethlehem**.

Take a moment to list a few of your favorite relatives and how they're related to you.

Name	Relation to You
1.	
2.	
3.	
4.	

> Boaz took ten of the elders of the town and said, "Sit here," and they did so.
>
> Ruth 4:2

These elders act as **judges**. Boaz is doing everything by the book. He knows the **law** and he's abiding by it.

Describe a time when you tried to skirt around the law (an actual law of the land, a household rule, a school policy, a rule of church camp or youth retreat, etc.), but it didn't work.

_____

_____

_____

_____

Most laws and rules were created for our protection. Of course there are a few unjust laws, such as those that prohibit Christians in certain countries from proclaiming their faith. Can you think of any other unjust laws?

_____

_____

_____

_____

Think about a few of the laws of our land. List three laws that serve to protect you.

1. _____

2. _____

3. _____

It's always wise to obey God's laws. Check out Psalm 119:24. How does David (the psalmist) feel about God's laws (or statutes)?

_____

_____

Take a moment to write God a text message asking him to help you learn to love his laws.

To:

Type to compose   Send

Susie Shellenberger

Now take a peek at Psalm 119:33–34:

Teach me, Lord, the way of your decrees, that I may follow it to the end. Give me understanding, so that I may keep your law and obey it with all my heart.

What does David want to learn?

_____

_____

What is he committed to doing after he learns this?

_____

_____

Look at Psalm 119:54:

Your decrees are the theme of my song wherever I lodge.

David loves God's laws (decrees) so much that he sings about them. Why do you suppose he loves God's laws?

_____ a. He doesn't want to go to jail.

_____ b. He knows if he could please God by following the laws, they would also keep him out of trouble.

_____ c. He was running for mayor and had to memorize all the laws.

_____ d. He wanted to impress those around him who were in the police force.

Question to Ponder

What benefits will _you_ experience from following God's laws (commands, decrees)?

_____

_____

_____

_____

_____

_____

_____

_____

_____

_____

_____

BITE #2

Then he said to the kinsman-redeemer, "Naomi, who has come back from Moab, is selling the piece of land that belonged to our relative Elimelek. I thought I should bring the matter to your attention and suggest that you buy it in the presence of these seated here and in the presence of the elders of my people. If you will redeem it, do so. But if you will not, tell me, so I will know. For no one has the right to do it except you, and I am next in line."

Ruth 4:3–4

It may **seem** as though Boaz is acting flippant about becoming Ruth's kinsman-redeemer. It **sounds** as though he doesn't care if this other man claims his right. But Boaz actually has a keen **strategy** in mind. **Things aren't as they seem!**

There will be several times in your life when you won't understand the ways of God. God never asks you to understand; God simply wants you to obey.

Our minds are limited and human. We have a hard time understanding God's logic. Match the following:

1. The last will be _____ (Luke 13:30).

2. To be great, you must be a _____ (Matthew 20:26).

3. Whoever loses his life will _____ it (Matthew 10:39).

4. The first will be _____ (Luke 13:30).

5. The strong will be made _____
    (1 Corinthians 1:27).

   a. last

   b. weak

   c. servant

   d. first

   e. find

(You can find the correct answers at the end of BITE #2.)

Grab your Bible and turn to John 14:21. According to this Scripture, what will you do if you love God?

_____

_____

_____

_____

And what benefit will you reap?

_____

_____

_____

_____

_____

You don't have to **understand** God's ways to **obey** God. Look at Isaiah 55:8:

> "'For my thoughts are not your thoughts, neither are your ways my ways,' declares the Lord.

We may never fully understand God's ways until we get to heaven. Let's continue in Isaiah. Read 55:9. What are God's ways and thoughts higher than?

_____

_____

_____

_____

Again, we may not always understand God's ways, but with God's help we can learn to trust and accept **without** understanding! Take a moment right now to ask God for **faith** and spiritual **maturity** to accept God's ways without having to understand them.

(Answers to the quiz on p. 190: 1: d. first; 2: c. servant; 3: e. find; 4: a. last; 5: b. weak)

BITE #3

At first glance in the Scripture, we don't **understand** the ways of Boaz. We have to continue reading to see his **strategy**.

Thus far Boaz hasn't even mentioned **Ruth**, though she's the main focus of his **interest**. He's only brought up the fact that Naomi has **land**. The law stated that **property** had to be redeemed before a person could be redeemed.

"I will redeem it," he said.

Ruth 4:4

Obviously Naomi's relative is trying to do the **right** thing. He must have been a **generous** man to want to purchase the land and give it back to Naomi so she wouldn't have to wait until the Year of Jubilee. He can be **commended** for that.

Boaz probably had a **knot** the size of a mountain in his stomach when he heard those words. But he'd also thought ahead. He knew this was a **possibility**. So he presents the rest of the scenario.

Then Boaz said, "On the day you buy the land from Naomi, you also acquire Ruth the Moabite, the dead man's widow, in order to maintain the name of the dead with his property."

Ruth 4:5

Uh-oh. Trouble for the relative. He didn't know there would be a **marriage** if he claimed the land. But now he realizes that to redeem the land, he'll also have to marry **Ruth**.

Notice how Boaz describes Ruth: "the Moabite." Grab your Bible and turn to Deuteronomy 23:3.

Who was not allowed into the congregation of the Lord?

_____

_____

_____

According to the law, if this relative brings Ruth into the assembly of the Lord, he'll be jeopardizing his own **property**. That's a big chance to take.

Boaz doesn't think twice about taking such a **risk**. He is in love with Ruth. He's willing to do whatever it takes to redeem her—**at any cost**!

How does this compare with Christ's love for you and the price he paid for your soul?

_____

_____

_____

_____

Think about it: Christ not only loves you; He's *in love* with you! Pray that he will help you fall more in love with him every single day of your life.

> At this, the kinsman-redeemer said, "Then I cannot redeem it because I might endanger my own estate. You redeem it yourself. I cannot do it."
>
> Ruth 4:6

The man may already have a family. But even if he jeopardizes his own **property**, can you imagine how happy Boaz must feel? At this moment he knows he will get to be Ruth's **kinsman-redeemer**!

Christ tells us that all of **heaven** breaks out in a giant party when someone gives their life to the Lord. The angels, the saints—everyone **celebrates** big-time! Nothing makes God **happier** than for people to surrender to him.

Question to Ponder

God will probably have a "welcome home" party for you when you arrive in heaven. Describe what you imagine that may be like.

_____

_____

_____

_____

The only way through life is to go through, to grow, to learn. Life was never meant to be a museum. The way out is through, to be a part of the human experience.

But to succeed at all — to be on blinks out on the other hand gives the illusion. You see the beginning is the end, but there is no ending, and maybe there is no certain and start.

Question to Ponder

What will your big love become then that you sleep, eat, and grow in between? Could what breaks the may be this.

BITE #4

> Now in earlier times in Israel, for the redemption and transfer of property to become final, one party took off his sandal and gave it to the other. This was the method of legalizing transactions in Israel.
>
> So the kinsman-redeemer said to Boaz, "Buy it yourself." And he removed his sandal.
>
> Ruth 4:7–8

You might remember from earlier in our study, the **law** stated that if a kinsman-redeemer refused to help out his relative, the woman could **spit** on him and remove his sandal. Boaz doesn't spit on the guy, but he **does** remove his sandal. He's acting in Ruth's place. Technically, **she** should be there. She should be the one to go through all the legalities and details. But Boaz wants to take care of things **for** her. He takes her place.

Describe how Jesus has taken your place.

_____

_____

_____

Someday you'll stand before God for judgment. Because Christ will stand in front of you, the Father will see his perfect Son instead of your humanness. Imagine this conversation:

Father: "Why should I let her into my perfect kingdom? She has sinned."

Son (stepping in front of you): "Yes, Father, she has sinned. But I chose to pay the price for her. Because I died, my blood has erased her sin. She is cleansed. Her sin is no more."

Father: "Yes, my Son. When I look at her, I actually see you. Let her into my kingdom. We'll celebrate our love for her!"

What are your reactions to the above scenario?

_____

_____

_____

_____

Boaz stands in the gap for Ruth. Grab your Bible and turn to Ezekiel 22:30. For whom is God looking?

_____

_____

_____

Where does God want him to stand?

_____

_____

_____

Notice God doesn't say, "I'm looking for the **smartest** person in your state to stand in the gap. I'm searching for the most **popular** girl. I'm hoping to find the best **athlete** in your school to stand in the gap. I'm only looking for the most **qualified**."

Jesus didn't say that, did he? He's looking for **anyone**! Anyone who's simply available will do!

Are you totally available to Christ?

_____ a. I'm available most Sundays.

_____ b. Yes, I'm available. I'll do anything he asks me.

_____ c. I'm available for a price.

_____ d. I'm available if my friends are.

God wants your availability. All through Scripture it's obvious God doesn't always choose people with **ability**. God always chooses people with _availability_!

God doesn't always choose the qualified; he qualifies those he chooses. Don't be afraid of what you can't do for God. If you're simply available, God will take care of the rest.

Ruth, in faith, claims Boaz as her kinsman-redeemer. He takes care of everything else. Jesus can do **mighty** things through the person who's totally **available** to him!

In which areas of your life do you find it most difficult to be available for God?

Write a letter to Christ that either asks him to help you become totally available to him or pledges your total availability to him.

BITE #5

Then Boaz announced to the elders and all the people, "Today you are witnesses that I have bought from Naomi all the property of Elimelek, Kilion and Mahlon. I have also acquired Ruth the Moabite, Mahlon's widow, as my wife, in order to maintain the name of the dead with his property, so that his name will not disappear from among his family or from his hometown. Today you are witnesses!"

Ruth 4:9–10

First Boaz redeems the **property**; then he redeems **Ruth**. He does this because he **wants** to. **He's in love with her!**

Christ didn't die for you because he had to. He **willingly** went to the cross because he loved his **Father** and wanted to do his will and also because he loved (and continues to love) **you**!

When you think about it, Christianity is really . . .

_____ a. a big fairy tale.

_____ b. available only to athletes.

_____ c. a wonderful love story.

_____ d. possible only if you live in Texas.

Susie Shellenberger

Have you ever thought of Christianity as a love story? Christ has pursued you with a passion since the day you were created! How does this make you feel?

_____

_____

_____

> Then the elders and all the people at the gate said, "We are witnesses. May the Lord make the woman who is coming into your home like Rachel and Leah, who together built up the family of Israel. May you have standing in Ephrathah and be famous in Bethlehem. Through the offspring the LORD gives you by this young woman, may your family be like that of Perez, whom Tamar bore to Judah."
>
> Ruth 4:11–12

It sounds as though the elders (judges) are . . .

_____ a. really angry.

_____ b. really crazy.

_____ c. really mean.

_____ d. really happy.

The elders are **rejoicing**! They're happy that a foreigner **left** her pagan gods and put her faith in the one true God. They know she has made a **sacrifice** to trust the Lord. They realize she didn't come to Bethlehem to chase guys. **Her priorities are right.** She's obviously a woman of good character and willing to work hard to provide for herself and her mother-in-law. And through it all, she hasn't become **bitter** or longed for her old life. **She's consistent.**

What have you left behind to follow God? (Attitudes, friendships, relationships, habits, etc.)

_____

_____

_____

_____

_____

_____

Name at least three people who rejoice with you in your faith.

1. _____

2. _____

3. _____

Throughout Scripture Christ refers to the church as his . . .

_____ a. sore spot.

_____ b. bride.

_____ c. joke.

_____ d. thorn in the flesh.

Boaz takes Ruth as his bride. Christ also receives *you* as his bride. To become his bride, what kind of *covenant* is necessary?

_____

_____

_____

Take a moment to write out your vows to Christ as you pledge to be his forever.

_____

_____

_____

_____

_____

BITE #6

So Boaz took Ruth and she became his wife. When he
made love to her, the LORD enabled her to conceive, and
she gave birth to a son. The women said to Naomi: "Praise
be to the Lord, who this day has not left you without a
kinsman-redeemer. May he become famous throughout
Israel! He will renew your life and sustain you in your old
age. For your daughter-in-law, who loves you and who is
better to you than seven sons, has given him birth."

Ruth 4:13–15

Naomi needs a guardian to carry on the line of her
deceased husband, Elimelek. Ruth needs a guardian to
provide for her. You need a guardian to redeem you. But
there are millions of others living without hope, without
purpose; they, too, need a kinsman-redeemer.

Name three people you know who need to be redeemed.

1. _____

2. _____

3. _____

Take a moment right now to pray for each of the people
on your list. Ask Christ to reveal how you can make them
aware that he wants to **redeem** them.

Then Naomi took the child in her arms and cared for him. The women living there said, "Naomi has a son!" And they named him Obed. He was the father of Jesse, the father of David.

This, then, is the family line of Perez:

Perez was the father of Hezron,

Hezron the father of Ram,

Ram the father of Amminadab,

Amminadab the father of Nahshon,

Nahshon the father of Salmon,

Salmon the father of Boaz,

Boaz the father of Obed,

Obed the father of Jesse,

and Jesse the father of David.

Ruth 4:16–22

We learn that Ruth later gives birth to a **son**. This is Naomi's **grandson**. She rejoices in him and lays him in her lap. She probably loves being a **grandma**! What a journey Naomi has experienced. She went from being part of a great family living in the **city of bread** and the **house of praise** to living in the garbage dump.

While in the **dump**, she grieved the death of her husband and two sons. When she returned to the city of bread, she returned with only *one* daughter-in-law. Her land wasn't even her own anymore. But God provided for her. God **redeemed**!

And what a **journey** Ruth has had. She had to face the death of her husband before she'd been able to give birth. She left all that was familiar and placed her faith in a God she couldn't see. She trusted the God of her mother-in-law and moved to Bethlehem.

She did backbreaking **labor** and gained the attention of a wealthy landowner who admired her **faith in God** and her priorities. God redeemed her through Boaz. God blessed them with children, and eventually the **King of Kings**—Jesus Christ—would be born of this lineage!

Jesus has the **power** to make good things come from seemingly hopeless situations. He has the **desire** to redeem us from our sins and continue a good work in us.

What in your life has been less than desirable but God has turned it into something beautiful or valuable?

_____

_____

_____

_____

_____

_____

BITE #7

GRAB A FRIEND

Major applause for you! You just completed the entire book of Ruth! Now grab a friend and discuss the following questions together.

@ I don't always understand God's ways, but I want to learn to accept them without understanding. I realize this takes spiritual maturity and faith. Has there been a situation this week in which I demonstrated (or should have demonstrated) spiritual maturity and faith even though I didn't fully understand?

@ Was there a time this past week when I should have been more observant of the law (or rules) around me? Or was there a time I did what was right according to the law (or rules) though I may not have agreed with it?

@ Who are some relatives I need to connect with? Remind them I love them? Send a note to? Encourage?

@ How have I demonstrated my love for Jesus by obeying him?

Susie Shellenberger

Memorize It!

Try to memorize this verse with your friend and say it to each other the next time you get together.

"He will renew your life and sustain you in your old age."

Ruth 4:15

Journal

Okay, S.P.G., this is your space to record thoughts, prayers, and questions you may have pondered as you completed this final section. Some ideas to include:

@ List your prayer requests. (Later, as God answers them, go back and record the date when God answered your prayer.)

_____

_____

_____

@ Copy down any verse we studied in the previous chapter that you don't understand. Then let this be a reminder to ask your parents, Sunday school teacher, pastor, or youth leader about it.

_____

_____

_____

@ Jot down what stood out the most from this chapter.

_____

_____

_____

Ruth's mother-in-law (family) is so **important** to her that Ruth **listens** to her, **loves** her, and **obeys** her. **Which of those three do you find easiest to do with your family?**

_____

_____

_____

_____

Which of the three do you find most difficult?

_____

_____

_____

_____

It's God's will that you get along with your **family**. God is the **author of peace** and wants to breed unity in your family. There are two keys to listening to, loving, and obeying your family.

Loving God. Ask God to help you fall more in love with him every single day. As you do, you'll learn to see your family through God's eyes and to hear them through God's ears. If you truly love God, he'll teach you how to love your family.

Communication. Ruth and Naomi have great communication. They openly share with one another. If you'll communicate gently and honestly with your family, then listening to, loving, and obeying them will come a lot easier!

Now about **faith**. If you'll stop trying to figure it all out and simply accept Jesus even though you don't have full understanding of his ways, your faith will explode!

Faith isn't about understanding; it's about **believing** even though you *don't* understand. Check this out: "Now faith is confidence in what we hope for and assurance about what we do not see" (Hebrews 11:1).

Ruth demonstrated faith when she left her hometown for an unfamiliar land. She could have prayed this to God: "I doubt I'll get married in Bethlehem. I'll probably be seen as an outcast. I know I'm walking into poverty. But I believe Bethlehem is where you want me. I have placed my faith in you. So even though I can't see what's ahead, I'm going to trust you anyway. I'll follow you all the way, God!"

How can *you* demonstrate this kind of faith with regard to your future?

_____

_____

_____

_____

Do you realize the pressure that's been taken off of you? You don't have to understand and know the future! All you have to do is simply relax and follow God. This should make your faith **shine**! So relax, sit back, and **trust that God will bring** who you need into your life, in God's perfect timing!

Talk It Up!

Want free books?
First looks at the best new fiction?
Awesome exclusive merchandise?

We want to hear from you!

Give us your opinions on titles, covers, and stories.
Join the Z Street Team.

Email us at zstreetteam@zondervan.com
to sign up today!

Also—Friend us on Facebook!

www.facebook.com/goodteenreads

- Video Trailers
- Connect with your favorite authors
- Sneak peeks at new releases
- Giveaways
- Fun discussions
- And much more!